PRAY

Simply Breathe

52 Breath Prayer Devotions and

How to Create Your Own Prayers.

Ken L. Hagler

Copyright © 2021 Ken L. Hagler

All rights reserved.

No part of this publication may be reproduced, distributed, or transmitted in any form or by any means, including photocopying, recording, or other electronic or mechanical methods, without the prior written permission of the publisher, except in the case of brief quotations embodied in reviews and certain other non-commercial uses permitted by copyright law.

http://www.kenhagler.com

Credits:

Cover Design: Ken L. Hagler

Editors: Kathie Stasko and Meagan Nicole

Unless otherwise noted, scripture quotations taken from the (NASB®) New American Standard Bible®, Copyright © 1995 by The Lockman Foundation. Used by permission. All rights reserved. www.lockman.org

Dedication

To my children, Logan and Jillian.
You two inspire me always to be true to myself. May you run the race set before you the rest of your lives.

Acknowledgments

To Mark Cagle, Becky Hoskins, Susan Preece, Tony Shanks, Chris and Sherri Siegel, Anne Gratton, Kenn Pritchard, Shari McAninch, Anita Lynch, Kerri Casteel, Karen Davenport, Kay Wolfe, DeDe Reilly, Sarah Schwab, Michele Powers, Lee Brown, Jade Hayden, Mike Benson, Daniel Victorio, Bob Swan, Frank Bernat, Ruth Easterling, George Tomes, Jen Lea, Dina Russ, Hal Hall, Amanda Harmon, Mike Casebier, Whit Martin, Deb McCranie, Patrick Mewes, Paul Bradford, and Laurie Newman. Thank you.

To Scott Allan, my coach, the Self-Publishing School team, and ALL the amazing authors who are part of the SPS community! You rock!

To my editors, Meagan Nicole and the Rev. Kathie Stasko. Kathie, your notes on Facebook about this book kept it going even when I wasn't so sure. I can't thank you enough for believing in this project.

To Lauren. I am a writer and preacher but words come up short. I am so thankful we are doing this next "novel" of life together. Thank you for trying to understand who I am as a Christian, a pastor, and a writer. I can't always explain why I do what I do but thank you for loving me, believing in me and putting up with me. I couldn't do this without you.

Forward

Ken Hagler has been a colleague and friend for at least 20 years. I served as his District Superintendent, walked with him through the horrible disease and ultimate death of his first wife. I have preached in churches he served. I rejoiced with his finding the second love of his life and ultimately his move to Alaska. I know Ken.

Therefore, when I read Prayer: Simply Breathe I hear his voice and see his heart. You will as well. His authenticity and transparency is so very refreshing in a world that loves to elevate Rockstar preachers. Ken is a pastor with a pastor's heart.

The Discipline of the Breath Prayer is an easy discipline. Often we think of Discipline as an onerous, grit and gumption effort. However, here it is simply forming a habit which is freeing and life giving.

Simply Breathe in the wisdom of this work. Benefit from the journey of a fellow follower of Jesus.

Dr. Warren Lathem
President
Venezuela Now, Inc.
President Emeritus
Seminario Wesleyano de Venezuela

What Others Are Saying

"In the midst of life's noise; in the midst of too many things to do; in the midst of being pulled in too many directions comes this wonderful book on the practice of breath prayers. Ken Hagler has offered us a connection to God that is transportable to whatever our circumstances are. Pray these prayers, so skillfully written, and deepen your faith with every breath."

Rev. Kathie Stasko
Pastoral Care and Minister to Older Adults
Cumming First United Methodist Church
Cumming, Georgia

"From the first page, Ken's dedication to prayer in all its forms shines through. Reflecting on his own difficult experiences, he shares a practice that helped him through his worst times to help us through ours. This book will have a prominent place on my shelf to enhance my own spiritual practices and to share with my congregation, especially those who struggle to pray. With a pastoral heart for all people, Ken shares breath prayers that are so clear and inspirational that anyone can practice them. They're as easy as breathing."

Rev. Lisa Marie Talbott
Director of Connectional Ministries of the Alaska Conference
Pastor, Homer United Methodist Church

"In the Old Testament, one of the names of God is Yahweh. It is said with a lot of air, "yahhh-wehhh", mimicking the sound of a full breath cycle - inhale (yahhhh), exhale (wehhh). Try it. The ancient Hebrews believed that the name of God invokes the very energy and power that keeps us alive. It is the first word from the mouths of babies as they take their first breath, even before they learn how to speak. It is the last word that a dying person utters as they take their last breath. And in between is a lifetime of constantly, consciously and unconsciously, invoking the name of God. Pastor Ken Hagler, in his book "Prayer: Simply Breathe", taps into this age-old belief and practice, and gives it new expression in the discipline of breath prayer.

That this book was written during an extremely difficult time in Ken's life points to a profound truth in life. When we find ourselves in situations of distress, conflict or pain, our body's natural response is to tense up. Our breathing becomes shallow which then leads to a host other things - elevated blood pressure, headaches, loss of focus, back pain, which in turn lead to temper flare-ups or emotional breakdowns. And while the solutions to these difficult situations are not usually easy and may take time, all of them start with a simple step - pause, and take a deep breath. Breathe. Inhale. Exhale. Pray. Yahweh.

That this book is coming out during the middle of a global pandemic that attacks the respiratory system is not a coincidence but a welcome blessing. May this book be a reminder to breathe, literally and spiritually. May the next 52 weeks be a journey towards making prayer as normal and as natural, as routine yet as life-giving, as unprompted yet as essential as breathing itself."

Rev. Carlo A. Rapanut
Assistant to the Bishop
Greater Northwest Area of the United Methodist Church
SuperintendentAlaska United Methodist Conference

Table of Contents

Dedication iii

Acknowledgments iv

Forward v

What Others Are Saying vi

Table of Contents viii

Introduction: Just What Is Breath Prayer? 1

Chapter 1: It's You and God 4

Chapter 2: Start Breathing 8

Chapter 3: "Jesus, clean my heart and clear my mind so I can clearly hear you." 15

Chapter 4: "Help me to live grateful for the second chances you give, Jesus." 17

Chapter 5: "Spirit, still me. Search me. Show me. Shape me." ... 19

Chapter 6: "Prince of Peace, may my time, my work, and my rest honor you." 21

Chapter 7: "Help me act with justice and not judgment, Jesus." 22

Chapter 8: "Spirit of God, help me prioritize people over power and possessions." 24

Chapter 9: "Light of Life, I can't see. Be light to my feet." 26

Chapter 10: "Jesus, increase my faith and help my unbelief! 28

Chapter 11: "Jesus, be King of my heart, my head, my pride…my all."........30

Chapter 12: "Forgiving God, forgive my sins and help me forgive others."..32

Chapter 13: "Loving God, may all I do be pleasing to You."..........................34

Chapter 14: "Jesus, may everyone see your love in me." 36

Chapter 15: "Take me as I am, Lord, but make me more like Jesus."............38

Chapter 16: "God, be patient with me." 40

Chapter 17: "Jesus, have mercy on me in the midst of my mess." 42

Chapter 18: "God, Make Me a Giver of Your Grace and Goodness." 44

Chapter 19: "Spirit, help me live with joy today!" 46

Chapter 20: "Make me a maker of peace, Jesus." 48

Chapter 21: "May my love keep no record of wrongs, loving Lord." 50

Chapter 22: "May your peace that surpasses our understanding sustain my soul, Jesus." 52

Chapter 23: "Spirit of God, fill my empty soul with your light and love." 54

Chapter 24: "Gracious God, be patient with me, foolish child that I am." 56

Chapter 25: "Though I falter and fail, be faithful Jesus." 58

Chapter 26: "Spirit, fill my empty cup with grace overflowing." 60

Chapter 27: "Jesus, may your love be seen in my life." 62

Chapter 28: "Lord, free me from sins most sinister." 64

Chapter 29: "Prince of Peace, make me into the friend my enemy needs." ...66

Chapter 30: "Humble Savior, save my soul from vain things." 68

Chapter 31: "O God, how much more can a broken heart break? Begin something new!" 70

Chapter 32: "Good Shepherd, keep me from evil so I may follow your good ways." 72

Chapter 33: "Abba, Father, help me grow younger in love and wonder." 74

Chapter 34: "Loving God, make me able to love all people." 75

Chapter 35: "Prince of Peace, be my light and life in dark places." 77

Chapter 36: "Loving God, may your Spirit take root in my soul." 79

Chapter 37: "Be my strong deliverer, my Lord, my God." 81

Chapter 38: "Lord, make me mindful of moments of temptation and your grace." 83

Chapter 39: "Loving God, teach me to trust and keep me from harm." 85

Chapter 40: "In my shattered state my soul sits. Save me from sorrow and sin, Gracious Lord." (Psalm 62:1) 87

Chapter 41: "My God, my guide, make sure my next step." 89

Chapter 42: "Holy Spirit, quiet my mind so I might hear your voice." 91

Chapter 43: "Forgive me, Lord, so I can live forgiving." 93

Chapter 44: "This is your day, Lord. May my life show it." 95

Chapter 45: "Holy Spirit, speak clearly so I may hear and follow faithfully this year." 97

Chapter 46: "Lord, you know. Hear my every sigh." 99

Chapter 47: "Jesus, make me an attentive listener and a devoted follower." 101

Chapter 48: "Our Father, keep me on the path of righteousness." 103

Chapter 49: "O God, be Immanuel. Be with us. Be with me." 105

Chapter 50: "Guide my children in your ways, O God." 107

Chapter 51: "Holy Spirit, quiet my mind so I might hear your voice." 109

Chapter 52: "Jesus, help me bear witness to your mercy and love." 111

Chapter 53: "Jesus, open my ears to hear and eyes to see the least of these." 114

Chapter 54: "Spirit of God, abide in me." 115

Chapter 55: How to Create Your Own Breath Prayer 116

What did you think? 124

About 125

Introduction: Just What Is Breath Prayer?

What more is there to say about prayer that has not already been said? There are over eight-thousand books and counting on Amazon regarding prayer, and that is just regarding Christian prayer. For all the articles and books on people leaving organized religion, especially churches, it is amazing how much interest exists regarding spirituality and prayer.

I am a practitioner of the practices of prayer - I pray - I have been instructed in prayer - I have guided others in prayer - nearly every Sunday, I guide a congregation in prayer. Every day, I pray personally. I am a pastor and it is what I do.

I haven't always been a pastor and praying didn't always come easy to me. I did have what I believe were some encounters with God early on in my life. They were vitally important, but they certainly did not set the tone for me becoming a "prayer warrior."

For a long time, prayer seemed more a tedious work not the conversational connection to God so many have spoken about.

But then something happened. Something changed my understanding of prayer that gave me permission to pray in a way that was as simple and natural as breathing itself.

What was it that changed prayer for me? Simple. I discovered Jesus gave us more than one model for how to pray. Of course there is the Lord's Prayer, the prayer Jesus gave to the disciples when they asked Him specifically about prayer, but that isn't the only model for prayer Jesus gave.

I learned the Orthodox traditions of the Church have been praying this prayer for centuries, calling it simply "The Jesus Prayer." Using prayer ropes, they pray the Jesus Prayer in some variation that goes, "Lord Jesus Christ, Son of God, have mercy on me, a sinner." It is a prayer intended to be prayed, literally, as you breath.

Plain and simple, this is praying Scripture and praying the other prayer Jesus taught. Using a prayer rope or prayer beads, I would pray the Jesus prayer 33 times in a row (the traditional number of beads or knots). I found before long, I was praying this prayer without even realizing I was praying. It was a prayer so simple I found myself praying without ceasing as Paul challenged us in his letter to the Thessalonians.

A colleague later introduced me to the book *The Breath of Life* by Ron Delbene. Ron shares his own journey and the practice of listening to God and our spirit to create breath prayers. These are prayers, like the Jesus Prayer, that are prayers of no more than a phrase or sentence to be prayed as we breathe.

For me, this journey of prayer coincided with my late wife's battle with colon cancer. I created my own breath prayer in the midst of those difficult days that expressed my heart to God, and I prayed it over and over again. In time, I began to consider what other concerns and needs God had placed on my heart. I began to take time each week to listen and create a breath prayer for each week.

I began using breath prayers as a regular practice in 2016.. Each week I post to Instagram and Facebook these prayers in hopes of helping others be encouraged to pray more regularly and feel more freedom to pray from their heart.

This book is a collection of fifty-two breath prayers. With each is a short devotional intended for encouragement. You may choose to use this as a daily devotional, or you may find it more beneficial to begin your week with the devotional and then pray the prayer throughout the week. You might consider using an Orthodox prayer rope or Protestant prayer beads along with the breath prayer. At the end, there will be space for you to work on creating your own breath prayers. Turn the page and lets get started!

Chapter 1: It's You and God

You are unique. You are "it." You have "it." You are the only one who has your "it." There is not another person in the world like you, and there never has been and never will be another. It seems to me this makes you pretty dad-gum special as we say down south.

If you and I are so special, then God is pretty, dad-gum creative! I mean, if God isn't making clones of us all, then God is spending a whole lot of effort and energy to make each of us special. And if we think on that a bit more, it must mean God is interested in the uniqueness of each one of us and what we might make of our lives and the world we live in.

I am also under the conviction God is interested in each and every one of us. There is something one of my spiritual teachers, Roberta Bondi, once said that has stuck with me a long time. She said one day, "God doesn't just love us; God *likes us*! God *really, really likes us*!" Her point was the God of all creation wants to hang out with us and enjoy our presence. God wants us to laugh and play, and God enjoys it when we are enjoying God and the world made. God doesn't just tolerate us or put up with us and love us despite our failures. God *likes us*!

God likes *you*.

Now, let that sink in.

And I cannot help but think that if God is so interested in us all being unique and likes us, God must be interested in what is going on in us too. We live in this world through our mental, emotional, and physical selves, but there are many who believe there is a spiritual part of us too. There is a longing deep inside of us. The multitude of religions gives testimony to the search many human beings have been on, trying to understand this longing for God.

Prayer represents one of the primary things we do when it comes to seeking God. Praying is what we call talking to God.

I can remember praying back in 5th grade over a lost magic snake toy. It was a desperation prayer. I had taken it to school against the rules my parents had established. It was a time in my life that I had grown rebellious in a lot of ways. And maybe it was grace or God's way of sparking hope into my life, but the day after I prayed, the toy was found and returned to me. Kind of a silly story, right? But things that happen when we are young can make life-long impressions, and for me, it was the beginning of a journey with God that is continuing to this day.

While I might wish I could give you a list of prayers God has answered in miraculous ways, I can't. On one side, I can look at this prayer of a fifth grader that God seemed to answer, and on the other side, I can look back on the prayers for healing for my late wife that God seemed to not answer.

Prayer is the act of turning our mind, our emotions, our body, and our spirit to God. The practice of prayer is a practice of laying aside our worldly worries and cares and turning our whole attention to the presence and heart of

God. It doesn't mean we forget our concerns—for God does care about those—but we release them into the presence of God and trust God with them. In prayer, we encounter and converse with God.

Let's look a little more intently at the prayers Jesus gave. Jesus' disciples once noted that John the Baptist had taught his disciples how to pray so they asked Jesus to teach them. In response, Jesus gave them the prayer that today is called "The Lord's Prayer" or "The Our Father"

"Pray, then, in this way:
Our Father, who is in heaven,
Hallowed be Your name.
Your kingdom come.
Your will be done,
On earth as it is in heaven.
Give us this day our daily bread.
And forgive us our debts, as we also have forgiven our debtors.
And do not lead us into temptation, but deliver us from evil."
(Matthew 6:9–13)

But this was not the only thing Jesus had to say about prayer nor was it the only prayer Jesus gave to His disciples that is honored by Christian churches even to this day. Luke records a parable regarding a Pharisee and tax collector that gives us another prayer to consider.

He told this parable to some people who trusted in themselves that they were righteous and viewed others with contempt:
"Two men went up into the temple to pray, one a Pharisee and the other a tax collector. The Pharisee stood and was praying this to

himself: 'God, I thank You that I am not like other people: swindlers, unjust, adulterers, or even like this tax collector. I fast twice a week; I pay tithes of all that I get.' But the tax collector, standing some distance away, was even unwilling to lift his eyes to heaven, but was beating his breast, saying, **'God, be merciful to me, the sinner!'** I tell you, this man went to his house justified rather than the other; for everyone who exalts himself will be humbled, but he who humbles himself will be exalted." (Luke 18:9-14)

This prayer became what we know as the Jesus Prayer in the Orthodox tradition of the Christian faith. Jesus would go on to teach many things about prayer as did Paul and other writers of the New Testament. Through the centuries, the desert fathers and mothers, saints, pastors, monks, priests, professors, and popes have all expounded on prayer.

One of those, Bernard, cut to the core of what prayer really is, what it means and what it does in us. Bernard writes this:

"By prayer we focus the soul in God. And when we focus only on Him, we cut out the distractions of the world and see Him lifted up before the eyes of the soul. And in this state, the Spirit speaks in us so that we discern God's will - and by this, what is important to God becomes important to us."[1]

---

[1] David Hazard, *Your Angels Guard My Steps*: Bernard of Clairvaux, Minneapolis, Bethany House, 1998, pg 72.

Chapter 2: Start Breathing

There come times in your life when you need to launch out on your own. Think for just a moment about those times. When you started walking, you gained independence. When you got the chance to learn how to ride a bike, a whole new world opened up. In your teenage years, you may have learned to drive, and suddenly, you could go almost anywhere!

But there are times when we are more hesitant too. Times when we may be unsure of our decisions and freedoms. We may at times wonder about our college choices or our careers. Some will struggle with the decision about their marriage or having children. Many people do the same thing with faith and religion.

Hopefully, we come to a point in our understanding of faith and God where we do launch out on our own. Choices regarding attendance in religious services become *your* decision. Even your choice of the religion you practice becomes just that: your choice.

But if there is one thing most common across not only denominations but also many religions, it is some concept of prayer. Prayer, this practice of having a conversation with the Divine, seems to be so simple, yet there is a multitude of ways to express ourselves and listen to God. You may have found this to be the case. But there are also those who will define prayer narrowly. Their approach works for them, so they take it to heart and assume it works for everyone else the same way.

In my life, I have prayed and taught about prayer. I have both taught and used the PARTs model to pray (Praise—Admit—Request—Thanks) spontaneous prayers. I have also used the Lord's Prayer as a model. These are helpful.

Many of the books I have read through the years seemed to imply there were strict rules and *only* certain ways to pray. Some authors or speakers don't even imply. They just state their conviction. I have read about how I needed a "breakthrough" prayer, and if I prayed this way, sure enough, God would answer me (I've not found "breakthrough prayers" in any of my biblical studies though).

Quite a few years went by, and even as a pastor, something was missing from my times of prayer. A few years ago, I was introduced to a very biblical and very Christian practice of prayer.

Dr. Bruce Rigdon was a lecturer at a Five Day Academy of Spiritual Formation sponsored by The Upper Room Ministries. Dr. Rigdon spoke on the scriptural foundation and spirituality behind the Jesus Prayer and its practice in the Orthodox tradition of the Church. I began praying it, and it quickly became part of my life and routine. I also read and studied its history and the scriptural foundations of the practice too.

It truly began to change and transform my prayer life and ultimately my relationship with God. I also saw this practice begin to show the fruits of the Spirit in my life. A few years after the Jesus Prayer became my practice for prayer, my late wife, Heather, was diagnosed with colon cancer. I had no idea at the time how significant these changes would become in my faith life.

Later, while reading Marjorie Thompson's book *Soul Feast*, I came across her description for the "Prayer of the Heart." She gives an introductory understanding of the Jesus Prayer but does not stop with this. It was in this section I was introduced to the "breath prayer." Had she not given some better explanation, I might have tossed the idea out. I followed her writings to the books of Ron DelBene, the pastor and author who coined the term "breath prayer."

For us, breath has a singular meaning in English. In Hebrew (the language of the Old Testament), breath is *ruach* and has two meanings. It means "breath," but it also means "spirit." The connection was not hard for me after this point. Not only was I praying the Jesus Prayer in my daily prayer, but I also began listening more intently for the deeper desires and cry of my own heart as I took time to both pray and breathe.

In the winter of 2016, right after the oncologists informed us there was nothing more they could do for Heather, I began to listen even more intently for God even as I wrestled with God over the situation. I longed to say and pray anything to help with the pain and struggles I was facing and to pray for Heather. I kept listening and wrestling.

On February 8th, I posted my first breath prayer and the words that follow: "Jesus, have mercy and grant me comfort."

I have written a number of times about the Jesus Prayer on my blog. It truly deserves more reflection from me as it has become my crutch…no…make that… my staff for it supported me long before the wounds I have since taken. But the form of prayer it has given birth to is equally important and something I feel called to share on in the days ahead.

Here is my first breath prayer: Jesus, have mercy and grant me comfort. It was birthed while I was praying the Jesus Prayer and the cry for mercy which I wrote about recently in another blog. As I prayed, there was another longing I began to sense in my soul which needed expression, it needed a word. It came from a totally different breath prayer from a few weeks before: comfort.

"Having just done a funeral and spent time with the stories of so many other caregivers, I was worn down. Weary. Maybe even a bit battered as well. Ever been in that place? Maybe from a relationship? A situation at work? A conversation at home? The isolation of family who have excluded you? Yeah, I suspect many have been there in different ways.

"The beauty and solace (another rich word) of praying a breath prayer is in the repeating of it. No, not like that of the Pharisees that Jesus condemned for you don't do it out on the

street corner. You ponder it. Chew it. Savor it. Like hot tea or a coffee or cider. And you do it as many times as you need it. Silently or out loud. In the moment you need it. Mercy."

Since then, almost every week, I listen to my own soul and to the Scriptures for the cry of my heart or the Scripture writer's cry. I listen to the news and read reports of the day and seek to hear how the Spirit is still crying out. And then, I seek to form it into a breath prayer each week and post it across social media and collect them.

I hear people talk about how ritualizing practices take away spontaneity, that praying written prayers from others is impersonal. For some people, I have no doubt this is true, but not everyone finds this to be *the* truth. The longer I reflect on the idea, the more I think these kinds of ideas come out of what stage we are in our lives. To some degree, this comes from our maturing as adults and as followers of Jesus Christ.

By making our reality everyone's reality, we miss out on other prayers, on God's words given to us through others. One example is how we think about the names of God. The idea of "our Father" or "our God" helped me to bridge the gap regarding our connection to the Church when I pray. God is not "my" God but "ours" because we are the body of Jesus Christ.

The more I look and meditate on breath prayers and read those prayers others have written, I often see and hear echoes of Scripture. Could this be part of the idea the psalmist had in mind when writing the words, "I have treasured Your word in my heart, So that I may not sin against You" (Psalm 119:11)?

Our prayers, whether our own or ones we adopt as our own, can tell us something about how we are in our heart, in our soul. I know many of my prayers reflect my own inner pain and desire for God's comfort. Much like journaling or practicing a form of personal examination, breath prayers give me an indication of my own soul health.

So, as you use these breath prayers, let them be like a thermometer for your soul. Pick one that seems to "fit." Each chapter starting at Chapter 3, is titled by a breath prayer. Pray it repeatedly for a few minutes if that fits your mood. Write it on a notecard and pray it in your car on the way to work. Make it a screensaver on your computer. Use prayer beads. Pray them as you cook, as you type, or as you exercise. The point, of course, is to let them be a prayer as you breathe in and out every moment of the day.

The purpose here is for *you* to pray these as your own and allow them to express your heart to God. God can handle our needs and knows them before we even say them (Matthew 6:8). Make them your own.

But don't let it end here either! After you have journeyed awhile, listen to your soul and God's Spirit. Begin to breathe for yourself. Listen to God, the still small voice and the yearning of your heart alongside God's. Start creating your own breath prayers,\ and start breathing new life and new hope into your faith!

It is time to start the journey. Turn the page, and let's go!

Chapter 3: "Jesus, clean my heart and clear my mind so I can clearly hear you."

On my list of least favorite things is unloading the dishwasher. I do not mind washing dishes, but I have a love/hate relationship with dishwashers. Why? Because sometimes they just don't do their job! Bowls are the worst because you can see the outside, which is usually spotlessly clean. Then you pick up the bowl and look inside and see the dishwasher failed at its job. Ugh. Sometimes I'd rather just take the extra time and wash it all by hand. Only when I am attentive to the task and results can I know for sure the job is done.

And Jesus says our souls are much the same: "Woe to you, scribes and Pharisees, hypocrites! For you clean the outside of the cup and of the dish, but inside they are full of robbery and self-indulgence." (Matthew 23:25)

Jesus addresses the religious orders of His day, but we would do well to pay attention to the correction Jesus gives to our lives. It is not your pastor or the author you read who is responsible for the state of your soul. How often do you "clean up your life" for the world to see but only show the outside? How often do you address the condition of your heart and soul? How often do you face your actions, your motives, and your own hypocrisy?

Jesus does not leave you wandering and meandering regarding your soul's condition. He is ready and willing to grant mercy, extend forgiveness, and make clean our hearts and minds. You and I must take the step of putting ourselves in the hands of God's mercy, asking for forgiveness, and partnering with the Spirit in prayer and reflection so we might have souls clean and clear.

Chapter 4: "Help me to live grateful for the second chances you give, Jesus."

"Then Peter came and said to Him, 'Lord, how often shall my brother sin against me and I still forgive him? Up to seven times?' Jesus said to him, 'I do not say to you, up to seven times, but up to seventy times seven."
Matthew 18:21-22

You lied. It wasn't a big one, just a little white lie, and it won't hurt anyone. You shared a little bit of gossip. It wasn't a big thing, and in fact, it was your true opinion, even if it wasn't wholly true. You borrowed. You were going to give it back before anyone knew it was gone. But then you didn't, and now, it is too late.

Yeah, you don't want to admit it, but you've done things you shouldn't have. You regret it. The guilt is too much at times too. But if you come out and own up to it, you are afraid things just can't be put right.

The Bible has a word for this: "sin." It is a word to describe the actions you do that miss the mark. Usually, we think about sin as the thing we do that breaks God's laws. Some of those things are things you do to God. Some of them are things you do to other people. But when you do it to other people, you do it to God too.

There is a secret though, and you need to hear it.

Whatever you've done, God isn't done with you. We learn from the psalmist about God's approach, "But You, Lord, are a compassionate and gracious God, slow to anger and abundant in mercy and truth" (Psalm 86:15). Jesus taught again and again that God is patient and grace-giving. God gives second, third, and fourth chances. Jesus said that math in the Kingdom of God is more than we can imagine-rather than forgiving just seven times, it is more like seventy times seven (Matthew 18:21–22). In other words, forgiveness is without end.

Pray to live more grateful this week for all God has offered. Pray knowing God isn't done with you. Not now and not ever!

Chapter 5: "Spirit, still me. Search me. Show me. Shape me."

"Be still, and know that I am God…" – Psalm 46:10a, KJV

Still me. In a world full of demands and responsibilities, finding time to be still is a rarity. Teachers of spirituality and meditation often refer to "mindfulness," but the history of Judeo-Christian faiths indicates this is part of the need of your soul. Not only do you need to give yourself permission to be still, it is also part of what God calls you to practice.

Search me. Your own heart can be deceitful and betray you, warns Jeremiah 17:9. What are you to do then when you betray yourself? Seek God's guidance to make you more like Jesus.

Show me. Maybe the hardest thing you and I deal with is criticism, but the feedback is needed. Even so, for you to progress on the spiritual journey, you need to become more aware of your weaknesses and where wickedness and deceitfulness arise and taint your life and decisions. You don't just need God to search your heart; you need God to reveal to you your true nature (Psalm 139:24).

Shape me. It isn't surprising that the writers of the Bible refer to the work of potters with clay when talking about the spiritual journey (see Jeremiah 18). Any one of us can pick up clay and make it into something that other people can identify: a snake, a pot, or a dog, for example. You were created in the image of God and called to be like Jesus. Isaiah 64:8, notes, "…we are the clay, and you are our potter; and all of us are the work of your hand." God is on your side and working for your good!

Chapter 6: "Prince of Peace, may my time, my work, and my rest honor you."

"Remember the Sabbath day, to keep it holy." – Exodus 20:8

Sometimes, your week gets out of hand. The kids have a bad morning and are late getting to school. That makes you late getting to work. The coffee is cold, and from there, it seems the whole week is off. You hope the weekend will change it all, but by the time you make it there, the kids have school assignments, you have a honey-do-list you're behind on, and the car still needs the oil changed.

Admit it. You've had those weeks. I suspect you have even had more than one of those weeks. They are hard.

Author and doctor, Matthew Sleeth writes, "I don't try to define what rest is for a person, but I ask you to figure out what work is for you, and don't do it one day out of the week.[2]" Funny that those words kind of sound like what God is telling you in Exodus 20:8. You need to take time to rest.

Yes, you should work. Yes, you should be productive. Yes, you need to take time off to rest. All of your life has the potential to bring honor to God. As you pray this prayer, allow God to work in your work and in your rest.

---

[2] https://www.cnn.com/2013/01/11/health/sleeth-take-day-off/index.html

Chapter 7: "Help me act with justice and not judgment, Jesus."

"Therefore, return to your God, observe kindness and justice, and wait for your God continually." Hosea 12:6

No sooner is someone in the news than we begin to talk about them and the accusations. In no time at all, judgment is passed on whether the person is guilty or innocent. Then you have to go onto websites to try and fact-check whether what is being reported is true or not.

It seems we human beings are far too quick to rush to judgment rather than seek justice.

When we look at the gospel stories, we find judgment being passed on Jesus over and over again. Jesus was judged for healing on the Sabbath. Jesus was judged for eating with sinners and prostitutes. Jesus was judged for blessing children. It seems like Jesus was judged for everything he was doing.

Yet Jesus did not pass judgment on those who accused Him. On the cross, He cried out to God to act with mercy on those who condemned Him and crucified Him. How I wish I could say I would do the same, but I'm fairly sure I can't. But there is hope, and there is optimism in the words of the prophet Hosea.

As you pray this prayer, keep in mind the image of Jesus on the cross and His call for mercy. Take each moment as it comes and return always to God.

Chapter 8: "Spirit of God, help me prioritize people over power and possessions."

"One who is gracious to a poor man lends to the LORD, And God will repay him for his good deed." Proverbs 19:17

There is no shortage of news related to those in power. Not long ago, there was a television program dedicated to the *Life Styles of the Rich and Famous*. Some of the most popular television shows today are obsessed with families who are powerful and influential. Our society measures your value and worth by power and possessions.

God sees things differently.

God doesn't see caring for the poor as an issue of charity. God views caring for the poor as an act of love comparable to His own acts of love for each and every one of us. In each person, there is the image of God.

In an odd parable, Jesus commends a shrewd manager for canceling out debts owed to the owner of the business he was worked (Luke 16:1-13). At first, it might seem like he was robbing from the owner, but in essence, he was giving up his own salary to build stronger relationships with these clients. He was putting a priority on relationships over riches.

You have only so much time on this planet. You can do anything you want to with the time you are given. God does not leave you and me to guess what kind of life is pleasing to Him. It is a life that prioritizes people over stuff. Sometimes, it is difficult for you and me to see it. As you pray this prayer, may you come to live a life that prioritizes people in need over stuff.

Chapter 9: "Light of Life, I can't see. Be light to my feet."

"Then Jesus again spoke to them, saying, 'I am the Light of the world; the one who follows Me will not walk in the darkness, but will have the Light of life.'" – John 8:12

"Your word is a lamp to my feet And a light to my path." –Psalm 119:105

I have spent a lot of time out in the woods hiking and camping. I can't tell you the number of times I have tripped in the dark, but I can tell you that it is a good idea to have a flashlight with working batteries!

The invention of the light bulb changed our world. Our work hours are no longer limited to the times in the day when the sun is up. You can drive your vehicle all night long if needed. Lights make it possible for planes to be able to be seen and to land in the dead of night.

In the time the Bible was written, there were no electrical lights. Oil lamps were a primary source of light at night. The light of a lamp, while not as powerful or effective as our electrical lighting today, still provided people the ability to see in the dark.

Throughout history, darkness has been associated with ignorance and evil. This isn't just true of the Bible. Both intelligence and faith are commonly related to light and lamps. The Psalm writer refers to God's Word as a lamp and light. Later, in the New Testament, Jesus is referred to as the Word of God (John 1) and says Himself that He is the light of the world.

We live in a world where darkness and evil sometimes seem to have the loudest voice, and goodness and love are covered by evil and hate. In your own life, you may find times when you too are confused and tripped up by darkness. There is light and there is one, Jesus, who is a light to your life. Call on Jesus in this breath prayer and call on Him to be a light for your life.

Chapter 10: "Jesus, increase my faith and help my unbelief!

"Immediately the boy's father cried out and said, 'I do believe; help my unbelief!'" – Mark 9:24

You have had it happen, no doubt, when things did not go as planned in your life. You may have suffered from an illness, lost a job, been at odds with your spouse, or dealt with a catastrophe that caused you to lose heart, lose courage, and lose your faith.

You are not alone.

Jesus came across a man who had been confronted by a demon possessing his son. As a parent, it is hard to imagine something so heinous and awful! It seems foreign to our ears, doesn't it? But if you think about something terrible happening to your child or loved one, then you can imagine how this dad must have felt. If you read the entire text of Mark 9:17-25, you find this demon would throw the child into fire and water.

When I read the text, I don't think Jesus was surprised by the father's response. It seems to me, he is trying to make a point to the father—God is on your side, so all things are possible! This father needed to hear words from Jesus. You need to hear it, and I need to hear it too.

So, whatever you are facing that is causing you to despair, you are not alone. Just as Jesus came to this Father in his time of need and despair, Jesus comes to you and me too. You probably didn't think of these words from this father as a prayer. But remember, if prayer is a conversation with God, then this moment when Jesus and the father shared these moments are a prayer worth taking to heart and praying without ceasing.

Chapter 11: "Jesus, be King of my heart, my head, my pride…my all."

"Therefore Pilate said to Him, 'So You are a king?' Jesus answered, 'You say correctly that I am a king. For this I have been born, and for this I have come into the world: to testify to the truth. Everyone who is of the truth hears My voice.'" – John 18:37

I remember playing baseball and basketball as a kid. When any of us got distracted and committed an error or foul, the coach would inevitably yell, "Get your head in the game!" Watching athletes play their sports, I think one of the things separating professionals from amateurs is their focus. They keep their head in the game. Their head and heart are dedicated to the goal at hand.

If Jesus isn't King of your life, you are missing the point of surrendering to Jesus' invitation. If Jesus isn't King of your life, then you are not a disciple, you are not a follower, and—dare I say it—you are not really a Christian. If your petty attitudes rule your life, if your political views determine your actions, or if your personal preferences keep you from loving Jesus first and loving others always, then Jesus doesn't have the primary voice in your life.

Jesus did not call you to follow an idea. Jesus called you to follow after Him.

The only person in the world you can change is you. There is no pastor or priest who can make the changes happen. They will certainly guide you, encourage you, and challenge you, but the work is done by the mercy and grace of God. The work truly begins when you stop being double-minded and welcome Jesus as the one in charge of your life.

It doesn't mean you become a robot with no aspirations. It doesn't mean you become a soldier and just follow orders. But it does mean you chose to care about the things and people Jesus cares about, and it does mean you learn the ways of Jesus.

It means you follow Jesus. Period.

Chapter 12: "Forgiving God, forgive my sins and help me forgive others."

"And forgive us our debts, as we also have forgiven our debtors and do not lead us into temptation, but deliver us from evil. For if you forgive other people for their offenses, your heavenly Father will also forgive you. But if you do not forgive other people, then your Father will not forgive your offenses." – Matthew 6:12-15

"Oh, what a tangled web we weave, when first we practice to deceive," comes from the play *Marmion* by Sir Walter Scott. It fits well the context of the play, but it also fits all too well the nature of our lives.

It hurts when people lie to us. It ruins relationships. There is no question about the impact it can have, especially when it is intentional. A relationship damaged by any perceived wrong may never recover. I suspect that reading this has already brought back memories or events you'd like to forget.

However, we deceive ourselves when we think holding grudges and keeping a record of wrongs done to us is a good thing. An article in WebMD addresses one study on how holding grudges and not forgiving hurts our

---

[3] (Fillon, Mike, https://www.webmd.com/depression/news/20000225/holding-a-grudge-can-be-bad-for-your-health#1, February 25, 2000).

overall health. People struggling to forgive sweated more, had higher blood pressure, and were visually more distressed.[3]

But Jesus was on to something when He taught prayer and spoke of forgiveness. We put a wall up in our relationship with God when we choose not to forgive. It hurts our soul and our ability to know and stay in love with God.

It may not make the hurt go away when you forgive. You may not even be able to forget what happened. But that is not what Jesus is saying. As long as you withhold mercy, you are saying to God, "I don't want your mercy." Ouch.

Take inventory of your life and relationships as you pray this prayer. Who are those you need to forgive? What grudge is keeping you from God?

Chapter 13: "Loving God, may all I do be pleasing to You."

"For this reason we also, since the day we heard about it, have not ceased praying for you and asking that you may be filled with the knowledge of His will in all spiritual wisdom and understanding, so that you will walk in a manner worthy of the Lord, to please Him in all respects, bearing fruit in every good work and increasing in the knowledge of God…" – Colossians 1:9-10

When an infant cries, they are communicating to a parent or caregiver or whoever is nearby to come help! When two people begin a dating relationship, they are aware of every aspect of body language and facial expression as part of communication. In my vocation as a therapist and spiritual director, what takes place is more than just me telling someone what to do. It is often a time of profound active listening and talking. When I have stood in public holding a "Free Listening" sign and the conversation is appropriately imbalanced (that is, when I am offering no opinion), it still requires mutual interaction.

The nature of relationships is they are a two-way street.

So is it with you and God. Are you unsure? Consider the stories in the Bible from Genesis all the way through to Revelation. There is a constant dialogue between God and people. In the Old Testament, it is often through the angel of the Lord that God speaks and people respond, but there are many occasions where God is on the scene and speaking directly to people like Noah and Moses. In the New Testament, we see God in human form in Jesus Christ—now that is speaking to God! The letters of the New Testament then tell us that God speaks through the Holy Spirit in our day.

God is interested in you! So contrary to opinions, the idea of a faith being merely about rules and regulations is far from what God desires. God's acts of love don't require us to do good but inspire us and empower us to a new life. The late bishop Reuben Job wrote it is an inspired life where you "do no harm, do good and stay in love with God!" I like the simplicity of that, don't you?

As you pray this prayer without ceasing, invite God to be part of all you do. Reflect on your day each day of the week. Really think about how you live and how your life has been pleasing to God.

Chapter 14: "Jesus, may everyone see your love in me."

"I have been crucified with Christ; and it is no longer I who live, but Christ lives in me; and the life which I now live in the flesh I live by faith in the Son of God, who loved me and gave Himself up for me."   Galatians 2:20

When I was a kid, I was involved in Boy Scouts. I learned early on when you put on the uniform of a Scout, people expect something more from you. If people learn you are a Scout, they look at your life and expect you to do your best to be trustworthy, loyal, helpful, friendly, courteous, kind, and on the list goes!

When people find out you are a person of faith, a follower of Jesus Christ, it is very much the same, or at least, they used to expect more. Sadly, today, people don't expect much more from Christians than they do from anyone else.

But being a Christian is not really about just being "good" or following a moral code or not doing bad things. No, something different is happening in us. Something far more significant than just trying to live a good life—God wants to be active and at work changing the world. God wants people in this world to be more like Jesus—people with the same radical, grace-filled, joyful, love Jesus lived!

The only way people are going to experience this love is to see first-hand this kind of self-sacrificing love running wild. It is only going to happen if you are loving: loving Jesus first and loving other people always. *This* prayer is all about *that* love running wild in you.

Chapter 15: "Take me as I am, Lord, but make me more like Jesus."

"Let's behave properly as in the day, not in carousing and drunkenness, not in sexual promiscuity and debauchery, not in strife and jealousy. But put on the Lord Jesus Christ, and make no provision for the flesh in regard to its lusts." – Romans 13:13-14

Winston Churchill, the famous prime minister of Great Britain, once said, "To improve is to change; to be perfect is to change often." I don't know much about Churchill's faith journey, but if he lived it according to this idea, he would be in agreement with what Paul is getting at throughout Romans.

Our lives are messy. Yours. Mine. All of us. Even in churches, we are people in conflict, and our selfish motivations and ambitions clamor for attention. We fail to see how our old self—our false self—has gained the upper hand in our lives. It regularly appears even in the place where we dedicate ourselves to God.

Over and over in the Gospel stories, Jesus met people where they were and cast a vision for where God wanted to take them. Saul was one of those kinds of people…a person just like you and just like me. Only, we likely haven't been caught trying to hunt down the followers of Jesus, right? This is what happened to Saul, but God didn't leave him full of hatred. Nope. God took him as he was, and God gave him a new vision (and new vision, literally). Then God set him on the course of telling and teaching and showing others the Good News of Jesus Christ!

You have your own story. It is one where at some point, you have likely come face-to-face with the messiness of your life and wondered or cried out to God, "What now?" Maybe this is where you are right now as you read today's thoughts. This may remind you of a time when you were in that kind of place. However you come to today's message, make this your prayer, and invite the Spirit of God to make you more like Jesus.

Chapter 16: "God, be patient with me."

"Then the Lord passed by in front of him and proclaimed, "The Lord, the Lord God, compassionate and merciful, slow to anger, and abounding in faithfulness and truth'" – Exodus 34:6

If there is a lesson that needs repeating in my life, it is my ongoing need to learn patience. On more than one occasion as a kid, I rushed through building models only to have my cars look more like something from a demolition derby than a new car showroom! Those were valuable lessons.

When I think of Jesus' parables, many of them had to do with plants and growth. There was the parable of the soils and the parable of the wheat and the weeds. Jesus talked about faith needing to be only the size of a mustard seed (Matthew 13:1-42). Having spent some time cultivating and caring for a few plants, one thing I know is you can't rush a seed to break the soil, and you can't push a flower to bloom before it is ready.

All those simple teachings combined with all we know of God in the Bible, we can be assured that God is not fast-tracking us to perfection! Read the whole book of Exodus, and you'll see firsthand that God was in no rush with the Israelites, allowing them to wander for forty years but never forgetting or ignoring them.

God provided. God guided. God remained present, and God remained patient.

Sometimes, it feels like we aren't where we ought to be in our faith. Our culture, our crowd, and even some in our church may make you feel like you are not far enough along on your journey of faith. If your spirit is feeling troubled by it, then this week, take it to God, and call on God to be patient with you just as God has been patient with all of those who have sought to follow Him faithfully.

Chapter 17: "Jesus, have mercy on me in the midst of my mess."

"Come now, and let us [a]debate your case," Says the Lord, "Though your sins are as scarlet, They shall become as white as snow; Though they are red like crimson, They shall be like wool.."' – Isaiah 1:18

I can remember so many times I disappointed my parents and made bone-headed decisions against their counsel. Many times, I found myself grounded in my room on days I should have been with friends. One of those times left me with a burned-up car engine. I learned valuable lessons from those times, including the importance of being humble because everyone makes mistakes.

Far too often, I think people have come to the conclusion that God just tolerates us and our mistakes. God really does not care much for people and the messes we make. The truth is that God is in the "do-over" business! He is the "Great Recycler!" From the beginning of the Bible all the way to this present time, God has been saying, "You are a mess, but I've got you. We'll get you cleaned up!"

Now, like a good, active parent, God intends to give us guidance and help along the way, *but* you *need* to hear this—your life cannot get so messy God is going to give up on you! Nope, not a chance! Think about what Isaiah says and imagine the last time you got a ketchup stain or a spaghetti sauce stain on a white t-shirt or pair of shorts—remember the work to get it out? When you come to God with this kind of mess, you need to hear Isaiah's words again and know God intends to take care of it.

As you pray this breath prayer to Jesus, think about the words Isaiah wrote regarding how God is looking at the mess. This is really what mercy looks like. The mercy is granted, and the mess is already in the rinse cycle!

Chapter 18: "God, Make Me a Giver of Your Grace and Goodness."

"Through Him then, let's continually offer up a sacrifice of praise to God, that is, the fruit of lips praising His name. And do not neglect doing good and sharing, for with such sacrifices God is pleased." – Hebrews 13:15–16

Abraham Lincoln was known for many things, but there was one thing about him that stuck with him through his life and beyond. What was it? His nickname: "Honest Abe." I'm sure there were probably a few "stories" he told in his life, but he had a reputation that stuck. He will always be remembered for his honesty.

What are you known for? What is your reputation? How would you like to be known and remembered? Most of us don't give that a whole lot of thought but the reality is, we are known for something by all the people we come in contact with throughout our lives.

It has often struck me that our world tends more often to focus on the evil and the bad rather than the good. Famous people and thought leaders are often known more for what they are against than what they are for. But God has something different in mind. He pays attention to our lives too, and there are things we can do to please God.

The writer of Hebrews notes how giving thanks and praise is important to God. So, when we share with others and do good, we are also "offering sacrifices," and it pleases God! So, rather than being defined by what you are against, why not consider living in such a way that people identify you with what you are for?

This week's prayer taps into this very thing—being someone who is known by what we give. It is also a prayer for us to be a living, breathing example of a life changed by God. Just as you have experienced God's grace and goodness, pray to become a person known for giving grace and goodness to others!

Chapter 19: "Spirit, help me live with joy today!"

" If you keep My commandments, you will remain in My love; just as I have kept My Father's commandments and remain in His love. These things I have spoken to you so that My joy may be in you, and that your joy may be made full." John 15:10-11

A good story keeps us on edge because we do not know how it will end. A good show will always take a break at the end of the season, leaving us guessing and wanting to know more come the start of the next season.

The story of Jesus is no different. In the days after Jesus' death, the disciples were confused and fearful over what had happened to Jesus. We know the end of the story today, but at the time of His crucifixion and death, the disciples were left questioning everything they had done and said over the previous years when they followed Jesus.

They would come to know the resurrection just as we do today! Even though life hits us with plot twists, we *know* that Easter brings with it the good news of new life. It gives us reason to have hope and joy.

Jesus said something interesting long before Easter though. He said that if we do the things He told us and showed us and keep doing them, then Jesus' joy would be in us, and we would be full of it!

So, when we care for our neighbors, we will know joy (Luke 10:25–37). When we love our enemy, we will know joy (Matthew 5:44). When we feed the hungry, joy will be in us (Matthew 25:35). When we turn the other cheek, joy will be in us (Luke 6:29). Jesus did not leave us wondering about how we might know joy but set us on the path by telling us how it will fill us.

As you pray this breath prayer, let the words of Jesus inspire you to live doing good. Because for us to live today and know the joy Jesus promises, we are to live as Jesus lived.

Chapter 20: "Make me a maker of peace, Jesus."

"Observe the blameless person, and look at the upright; For the person of peace will have a future." Psalm 37:37

"When the power of love overcomes the love of power, the world will know peace." Jimi Hendrix

At some point in our lives, many of us reach a point where we realize our ladder of success might be leaning against the wrong wall. When the day or time comes, it is likely you or I will have some crises, be it a mid-life crisis or a crisis of faith.

When I was a kid, I received a nameplate from my church, and under my name was Psalm 37:37. For my whole childhood, it hung on my wall until we moved in the middle of my junior year of high school, and it went into a box.

One of the popular things asked of Christians for a time was "what is your 'life verse'?" I had many that I would quote. But one day early on as a pastor, I found the nameplate in a box, and I realized I had been given a "life verse" years prior! Being a maker of peace is something we are each called to be as we follow after the one who is the Prince of Peace.

Why is conflict so much easier? Could it be we are so wired for ourselves that we fail to see the needs around us? You and I are being called to end conflict, and that may look very different than we think. It doesn't mean getting our way; it means getting it God's way.

As you pray this prayer, be attentive to the choices you are given in your relationships with those you come in contact with each day this week.

Chapter 21: "May my love keep no record of wrongs, loving Lord."

"[Love] does not act disgracefully, it does not seek its own benefit; it is not provoked, does not keep an account of a wrong suffered." 1 Corinthians 13:5

Be honest. You are keeping a record of wrongs, aren't you? In part, it is natural for us. When we are hurt, we protect ourselves and do not want to be hurt again. If there is a person responsible for it, we want to keep them at a distance once we feel the pain. Even when it comes from the people closest to us, we make note of the hurt, at least for a time.

We are quick to cry out for mercy when we have done something wrong, but out of the other side of our mouths, we cry for justice when we are the one wronged. We remember too well the offenses.

When it comes to God, we celebrate and give praise for the forgiveness He has given to us. It is the very nature of God to love us and forgive us. But what we celebrate in God, we fail to emulate toward one another.

Jesus told a story of a man who owed a great debt to a king, and the man begged the king to forgive. The king did so, but the same man went and demanded repayment of a small sum from another and refused to forgive the debt but kept a record instead (Matthew 18:21–35).

This week, begin to look into your own heart at the list of wrongs you are keeping, both the real and the imagined. As you pray, start forgiving and praying that the same love you celebrate from God becomes the love you emulate to others.

Chapter 22: "May your peace that surpasses our understanding sustain my soul, Jesus."

"Do not be anxious about anything, but in everything by prayer and pleading with thanksgiving let your requests be made known to God. And the peace of God, which surpasses all [b]comprehension, will guard your hearts and minds in Christ Jesus." Philippians 4:6–7

One of the most common illnesses of our time has become anxiety. There is a tendency in our society to feel things are out of our control, and this leads to anxiety. For some, we're born with the tendency, and for others, it seems to develop over time. I have found many times that anxiety comes from a false sense of control over things outside of our realm of influence. For instance, my children are adults now. They make decisions day in and day out that I do not have input on.

But anxiety is not new to us. In his words to the church at Philippi, Paul encourages those who are anxious to take those things to God. From this, we can come to receive a peace from God we can't understand. John Wesley, thr 18th-century preacher and writer, makes the observation that only God can give this peace, and none can understand it except for the one who receives it. Adam Clarke would write in his commentary, "It is felt by all the truly godly, but can be explained by none."

And when Philippians 4:7 speaks of "your hearts," it is what we understand our souls to be. It is where our personhood and passions lie. God wants us to experience something beyond a calm demeanor. It is more than just having no worries. It is a true assurance of the presence of God that frees us from the anxiousness that overwhelms and paralyzes us.

As you pray this prayer, what are those situations or relationships that cause you anxiety? Name them as they arise in your thoughts and go back to praying this prayer, making it your pattern.

Chapter 23: "Spirit of God, fill my empty soul with your light and love."

"Then the LORD passed by in front of him and proclaimed, 'The LORD, the LORD God, compassionate and merciful, slow to anger, and abounding in faithfulness and truth…'" –Exodus 34:6

I grew up in Mississippi. My first job was working for my dad, mowing lawns. After a while, I branched out with my dad's blessing and started my own small business mowing yards in my neighborhood. I actually did pretty well and had enough lawns in the summer to keep me busy most of the week. I remember drinking a lot of water, and I do mean a lot! But no matter how much water I drank, when the last drop was gone, I felt empty. I still wanted more.

Using prayer lists had been something I tried often and was part of my concerted pray focuses for intercession. These were all good and appropriate, but I often felt empty still. I wanted more of God, which led me to study and practice the more ancient practices of prayer in the Christian faith.

This prayer is an appeal for those times when the soul seems particularly parched or empty. The reasons could be many. It may be a particular season of life or following a loss or argument. It may come from an examination and conviction regarding a sin or overall sinfulness.

Here is the thing to note though. God's word to us in Exodus is that God is abounding with love and truth! God is full of these, *and* more than that, God is compassionate and gracious. God wants to give!

Meditate on those proclamations for a moment and throughout this day or week as you pray this breath prayer. We are not praying to just any deity, but One who knows our soul and our soul's remedy.

Chapter 24: "Gracious God, be patient with me, foolish child that I am."

"I gave you milk to drink, not solid food; for you were not yet able to consume it. But even now you are not yet able."   1 Corinthians 3:2

Looking back at old baby pictures of my kids and their first experiences with birthday cake always brings a smile to my face. Icing was all over their faces and fingers. Most of the cake was just mushed up and lots of wet wash clothes being used! I loved those days, but I loved the years to come after those too when my kids would eat and use the manners they had been taught.

I have to say that I am so thankful for the years that I have grown up in my faith and understanding of God too. But there are times—too often I might add—when I look inside my own heart and examine my motivations and find I am not quite as grown up as I thought. I harbor anger and resentment at times. I want my own way and demand my "rights" and in ways that make me cringe.

Sometimes, I read what Paul writes to the Christians at Corinth and think, *Yeah! How immature!* But on further examination of my own life and faith, I know those words are meant for me. A huge part of the spiritual journey is precisely this journey of understanding humility, after all! The early church mothers and fathers and the saints throughout the centuries consistently come to the conclusion that pride and being judgmental are sure signs of our lack of maturity in our faith.

This breath prayer leads us to consider where we really are in our faith and our dependence on God's grace. This is precisely where we ought to be putting our faith and trust after all, for Jesus revealed to us a divine parent who is not at all like us earthly parents and who is patient even when we find our faces and fingers still covered in icing.

Chapter 25: "Though I falter and fail, be faithful Jesus."

"If we confess our sins, He is faithful and righteous, so that He will forgive us our sins and cleanse us from all unrighteousness." 1 John 1:9

I can remember the first time I ever failed a test. It was a fourth-grade test on basic human anatomy. I forgot about it. I can't remember why. Does it matter now? No. I failed a few more tests along the way, and some of my class grades came out lower than I wanted to. But I graduated from high school and moved on.

What I do remember about that first failing grade was the disappointment and shame. Then I feared what it would be like to tell my parents. But their response was a surprise. They were comforting and caring, but they also made it clear, "You will fail sometimes. Don't make it a habit."

I faltered and failed a lot more since that day in fourth grade, but I learned a valuable lesson then. Namely, failing is not going to kill you. It will happen sometimes. And I learned not to make it a habit. I carried that lesson into a lot of areas of my life—in marriage and my vocation for sure. The hardest place though has been parenting because you, as a parent, don't get a grade. You don't really know how you are doing.

And this is true for the faith journey too. One of the most profound images in the Bible is that God is a Father (and thankfully the image of mother is there too). More specifically, Jesus refers to God as "Abba" or "Daddy," which is the loving and supportive image we long for as a child. We are adopted by this Daddy, and He knows all of our weaknesses and failings.

What we also are told is Jesus is faithful, and since Jesus is the image of this Daddy, we can be assured God is faithful. On our journey of faith, we need to remember it, to trust in the promise, and as we pray, take those times of faltering and failing to the One who is faithful…always.

In his first letter, John writes, "If we confess our sins, he is faithful and just to forgive us our sins and to cleanse us from all unrighteousness" (1 John 1:9, ESV). God remains faithful as we respond to the invitation and overture of Jesus to come and trust in the faithful promise to forgive. Own your shortcomings, stumbles, and failures this week as you pray this breath prayer. Let your focus be upon this important truth that Jesus is faithful, and let the faith grow in you!

Chapter 26: "Spirit, fill my empty cup with grace overflowing."

"Come to Me, all who are weary and burdened, and I will give you rest. Take My yoke upon you and learn from Me, for I am gentle and humble in heart, and YOU WILL FIND REST FOR YOUR SOULS. For My yoke is comfortable, and My burden is light." – Matthew 11:28–30

Growing up down south, a cup full of lemonade was something to behold and cherish. On a hot, scorching summer's day, none of us would waste a drop. We'd savor it all. When the cup was empty, it was always a disappointment, but we'd look forward to another as soon as we could get to the next house!

Truly, those cups were gifts of love from many moms making sure the neighborhood was having a great time. We never realized what those cups really were. Each was the way our moms said, "I love you, kids. Go have fun and don't grow up too fast!" To us, it just tasted great!

But we did grow up too fast. Only now can we look back and see the real gift behind each cup. We had moms and dads watching out for us, providing for us and guiding us. We know it now because many of us have our own kids and neighborhoods that we love and gift with lemonade and treats.

We surely did not deserve any of it. We were just kids playing hide-n-seek, shooting hoops, and riding bikes. We weren't out adding anything to society, but we still got this simple gift. There is a word for gifts we don't deserve: grace.

Today, I still find myself empty. Even if we love our work, it can wear you out. There are responsibilities at home and in our community that drain us. We give of ourselves to family and friends. We'll even do the same at church…and we forget Jesus promised to give us a burden that would be "easier and lighter" than what we carry.

Two of those gifts which come into our lives and are fruits of God's presence are peace and patience. They are gifts and ones that can make a world of difference in our lives. God doesn't have a desire for us to wear ourselves out but renew us and bless us in the most significant and intimate ways of our lives. If you feel empty, this is a prayer to guide us to grace—the multitudes of gifts God offers to you and me.

Chapter 27: "Jesus, may your love be seen in my life."

"Your light must shine before people in such a way that they may see your good works, and glorify your Father who is in heaven." - Matthew 5:16

When I do marriage counseling for couples, I usually will recommend one of two books after I do two sessions with a couple. One of those is *The 5 Love Languages* by Gary Chapman. Dr. Chapman identifies these "languages:" acts of service, words of affirmation, quality time, physical touch, and gift-giving.

Having used the book myself in my marriage and family and having worked with couples for many years now, I usually can ask a few questions to find out what each love language is for partners. But often reading the book and having conversations together, good couples will go through self-discovery about how to love their partner better and make significant changes. Sadly, not all will do this work.

What I am trying to get at though is not everything we say, do, or give is going to be interpreted as an act of love, even if it means this to us. My adult son might appreciate that I took time to fix him dinner, but he won't take it as a sign of love. If, however, we then eat together and watch a movie or show, this action is a sign of love because his love language is quality time, and he likes to hang out.

You and I need to take time to pray and ask God's guidance in our relationships to be able to show them love. Everyone is going to be different and respond differently. When we act toward others in a way meaningful to *them* and not ourselves, they will be able to truly "see" your act of love and give glory to God. As you pray this prayer, consider learning more about "The Five Love Languages" and applying its lessons to your life and how you love others with the love of God.

Chapter 28: "Lord, free me from sins most sinister."

"…and after being freed from sin, you became slaves to righteousness." Romans 6:18

Ever had the feeling of being trapped? How about being trapped *but* the reason was your own fault?

There were a few different ways my parents punished me for doing something wrong, but maybe none was more difficult to handle than being grounded. You could go to school, even drive to school, hang with friends, and learn all that was going on after school hours…but you couldn't go. It was even worse when you had a girlfriend! No phone calls, dates, nothing! Ugh!

Of course, this is a bit lighthearted. Some of you reading this have far worse experiences coming from run-ins with the law. You know what it is to be incarcerated for a few nights or a number of years. Some know what it is to have experienced addiction. These are all physical prisons, but there is a prison even more difficult that we face.

This is the prison you and I experience due to sin. We may not recognize being locked up here. Apart from morals or religious guidance, we act as though we are free and may even believe this to be the case. In truth, until we come to repentance, owning up to our failures and self-centered, self-absorbed focus, our souls—our true self—are just as much in a prison as any fence or addiction makes us.

We need help, and what we truly need is grace, the gift of God's free mercy pardoning us and giving us reason to hope and a vision for a future. The nature of sin is most sinister because we are born into it and cannot see it on our own. It surrounds us and dominates not only culture, government, and education but also influences religions and the people and clergy of God's Church.

None of us are immune to its constant attempts to ground us, but it is true all of us can be free and released from it and turn to a new way! Who we follow makes all the difference. There is no better time than starting to follow Jesus as Lord right now.

Chapter 29: "Prince of Peace, make me into the friend my enemy needs."

"But I say to you, love your enemies and pray for those who persecute you," - Matthew 5:44

My enemy.

Just who is my enemy?

In war, this seems straightforward. In politics, there are two or more sides trying to win popular opinion polls. Sometimes we might think of our business competitors as our enemy. But really, is there really someone out to get me? Is there someone or a group of people working actively to destroy me?

It seems kind of absurd, doesn't it? And yet, multiple magazines and publications have noted that in the 20th century, more Christians have died for their faith than in all the previous centuries combined. Depending on where you live in the world, a believer will experience these enemies in different ways. Some will actually seek to kill a follower of Jesus, but in another part of the world, a person's belief will simply be discredited or their faith ridiculed.

Does one fight back? Create a movement for respect? Appeal to Amnesty International?

Each response has a place, but Jesus challenges the Christian that in the end, one must seek to love those who wish us ill or evil because of our faith in Jesus Christ. That love ought to take a real form.

What action do we take toward our enemy? I'll admit that I sometimes need help with this, so I pray. With every act of violence in the world, I pray to become the friend my enemy truly needs.

Chapter 30: "Humble Savior, save my soul from vain things."

"I have seen all the works which have been done under the sun, and behold, all is vanity and striving after wind." Ecclesiastes 1:14

One of the great book and movie franchises is the James Bond series. I have seen every one of the movies and many of them more than once. The adventures, gadgets, and swagger of "her majesty's" number one secret agent are quite enjoyable. Like many things, 007 is a product of our culture and vanities.

What is portrayed is a cultural representation of who all guys want to be and who all women want to be with. He always gets away, saves the girl, lives an exotic lifestyle, and is given the freedom to do pretty much as he pleases. It is truly a life of vanity.

We are so tempted to seek after the prettiest, the most handsome, the sexiest, the richest, the most powerful, and so much more. Yet, over and over again, people who achieved success by these standards, find it just as easy to lose it all. The great equalizer—death—comes knocking on all of our doors.

To follow Jesus Christ means we are to take on the mantel Jesus did, the role of servant and a life of willful humility. Humility and vanity are two sides of our spiritual coinage. It is no wonder this prayer includes both. The road to humility will always lead to the death of vanity in our lives. The truth is also accurate in the opposite direction. To seek a life of vain things is to separate our souls from the path of Jesus Christ. As you pray this prayer this week, consider what vain things you are striving for and keep inviting Jesus to keep you on the path of humility.

Chapter 31: "O God, how much more can a broken heart break? Begin something new!"

"Behold, I will do something new, Now it will spring forth; Will you not be aware of it? I will even make a roadway in the wilderness, Rivers in the desert." Isaiah 43:19

There is an old saying that bad things happening in threes. I've always seen it the most when a celebrity dies or a tragic event happens. Watch carefully, and two other bad things will happen soon after. I don't know if it is true or just what I perceive, but it does seem to be true many times!

Sometimes though, it seems to happen in our own lives. The car breaks down, there is a roof leak, and a child gets sick. Sometimes, it is more overwhelming and may include the death of someone special, a job change, or a financial crisis all at once. These situations can be difficult to experience, and you may need help from a doctor, a counselor, or a support group.

It can be tempting to question if we have done something wrong and conclude God is punishing us. This often compounds our feelings, and in the end, it is likely not anywhere close to the truth of the situation. Bad things just happen. It is a part of life. Jesus noted for us that God "…makes his sun rise on the evil and on the good, and sends rain on the just and on the unjust" (Matthew 5:45, ESV).

Isaiah prophesied to the Jewish people to stop looking at the past and the failures that led them down the path to national defeat and exile by their conquerors. God uses Isaiah's words to point to what is to come: God is doing something new!

While God never changes, the coming of Jesus Christ did change the direction of humanity. The Good News of the Gospel remains good news to us today. In this regard, the Old Testament passages like Isaiah do apply to us as God's children today. God is always about doing something new, especially acting to redeem difficult situations in our lives. God is in the grace business and wants to restore life. Pray this prayer with hope knowing God is going to do new things in your life.

Chapter 32: "Good Shepherd, keep me from evil so I may follow your good ways."

"Let love be without hypocrisy. Abhor what is evil; cling to what is good." Romans 12:9

There seems to be no end to the evil that human beings will do to one another. The Holocaust perpetrated by the Nazis will forever be a blight on humanity. Apartheid in South Africa will be remembered in much the same way. That was the 20th century, but the 21st century has fared no better. Under the reign and demands of terrorist leaders, radical religious sects of have persecuted and killed combatants and innocents alike.

These are the big ones, but evil is available to us on a variety of levels. No one is immune to the temptations to act out. Oh, it may not seem to be evil at first. It may just be an innocent "observation" of another person's behavior, but from there, it may grow to full-on gossip and pridefulness in ourselves. It may be breaking "little" driving laws or ignoring a discrepancy at work.

You may not have grown up among shepherds, but it is a great image for us regarding how God watches over us. The shepherd protects the sheep from thieves and animal predators so they might grow. The shepherd also guides the sheep to new places to graze.

When it comes to needing protection, we are vulnerable to the spiritual realm and the temptations thrown our way by the evil one. Some Christians, it seems, remaining largely ignorant of spiritual things, and many times, we choose that route because we'd rather not live in faith. There are pagans have a greater respect for the spiritual than followers of Jesus do!

As you pray this week, consider and be alert to both the evil that is present around you and the ways God is guiding you in your growth. God knows the spiritual realm and the ways we grow best.

God desires the best for us, even if, like sheep, we can't see or comprehend it just yet!

Chapter 33: "Abba, Father, help me grow younger in love and wonder."

"Truly I say to you, whoever does not receive the kingdom of God like a child will not enter it at all." Mark 10:15

One of the most unique turn of events in life is when a person goes from being someone's child to being someone's parent. Becoming a father was, for me, a humbling experience full of hope and anxiety. I may have felt like a child, but I was now responsible for one (and later, two)!

Part of becoming a parent meant, in many ways, that I was a child again as well. I didn't know what I was doing! There was no book, no user manual, nothing that told you what to do in all of the situations you might face. I was just like my kids: new to this world!

When I read Jesus' words about becoming like a child to receive the Kingdom of God, I see it more clearly than I ever did before. Children trust their parents to care for them and watch over them as they look with wonder at the world. What children don't realize is that parents are looking with wonder at their kids and how they change our lives!

I wonder why it is so difficult for us to look with wonder at God's Kingdom. God, give us new vision!

Chapter 34: "Loving God, make me able to love all people."

"This is My commandment, that you love one another, just as I have loved you." John 15:12

It is hard to like some people, and the idea of loving them…well, that just seems a little much, doesn't it? I mean, some people aren't nice nor are they particularly pleasant to work with or be around. It does seem a little far-fetched that God would want us to love all people, right?

God did not come in human form of Jesus Christ looking for perfect people. God came looking for poor, perplexed, and pathetic people, and God's intent was and remains to transform them into people like Jesus and transform the world through them. So, yes, God does want us to love all people because this is the nature of God.

I particularly love how John's Gospel makes it clear not only in chapter 3 verse 16 but also in verse 17. Read it carefully:

> "For God so loved the world, that he gave his only Son, that whoever believes in him should not perish but have eternal life. For God did not send his Son into the world to condemn the world, but in order that the world might be saved through him." – John 3:16–17, ESV

God is in a rush to love us, not a rush to judge us. This is the example God has set for us and what Jesus invites us to do and the indwelling Spirit makes possible in us. A big part of the work of learning to love all people is turning a big part of the work over to God! This is what this breath prayer reminds us of this week: we become able to love all people because God already loves all people, and we're tapping into the source.

Chapter 35: "Prince of Peace, be my light and life in dark places."

"Then Jesus again spoke to them, saying, "I am the Light of the world; he who follows Me will not walk in the darkness, but will have the Light of life." John 8:12

When you consider your spiritual journey, it is common to think of the time before you had knowledge of the spiritual as a time of darkness. It is also common to consider yourself to be dead to spiritual things. When you came to a belief in God, it was like light was shone on your soul and you came to life.

In Matthew's Gospel, we find the writer referring to Isaiah 9:2 when he writes, "…the people dwelling in darkness have seen a great light, and for those dwelling in the region and shadow of death, on them a light has dawned" (Matthew 4:16, ESV). It is an image repeated again and again throughout Scripture.

I think it is valuable to also remember that darkness is the absence of light. Darkness cannot exist apart from light. And in the same way, we cannot know death without knowing life. True life comes from God. John's Gospel records Jesus saying, "I am the way, and the truth, and the life. No one comes to the Father except through me" (John 14:6, ESV). It is an incredibly comforting thing to be in relationship with a God whose very existence authors both light and life!

Probably the most difficult time to pray is when hope is extinguished and darkness and death suck the air out of the room. To pray along the lines of this prayer offers us the reminder of what God really brings to the table and how we might know the powerful peace to come from placing our trust in God.

Chapter 36: "Loving God, may your Spirit take root in my soul."

I am often amazed to see the places where plants and trees are able to take root. Walking on the sidewalks of a city block, it is not uncommon to find a dandelion or other weed taking root where a simple patch of soil can be found. As a backpacker, I have stood in awe of trees, upward of 3 inches in diameter, that have taken root and broken rock for its roots to become firmly established.

Then my attention turns inward more often than not, and I consider my heart and life. I can see where my own heart has become selfish and self-centered. In essence, I become like the concrete downtown or the mountain's rock face. It is a wonder anything could grow there!

Yet looking at those plants and trees tells us that life can take root in the hardest places.

When a person becomes a Christian, they invite the presence of God to come and dwell in their lives, in those dark and cold places. Paul questioned the Corinthian church about their faith when he asked, "Do you not know that you are God's temple and that God's Spirit dwells in you?" (1 Corinthians 3:16, ESV). So, why not take it one step further and invite God to put roots down and break up the "stone" in your heart and life?

As you pray this breath prayer, focus on the invitation for the Spirit to get the roots into your heart and life. Invite God to be a permanent fixture in your life, living and growing in holiness.

Chapter 37: "Be my strong deliverer, my Lord, my God."

"The Lord is my rock and my fortress and my deliverer, My God, my rock, in whom I take refuge; My shield and the horn of my salvation, my stronghold." – Psalm 18:2

As a kid, my friends and I often played "army." In every imaginary conflict, we had to escape to the safety of our fort or base. Usually, this was a tree house, swing set, or porch. There was always a place for us to take refuge.

The Jewish people of the Old Testament were a people all too familiar with war and conflict. They were not wanted as a nation. Where they were wanted, they were wanted as slaves and servants. When they spoke of fortress, shield, and stronghold, they meant it. They had a need for protection from real swords and arrows.

As a parent, I tried to insulate and protect my kids from the difficulties in the world we live in. My hope was always to prepare them to gradually face things as life got harder, but no matter how hard I tried, my protections have come up short. They need a strong Deliverer. And you know, I need one too.

The Psalm writer and this breath prayer are a crying out to God to be the One you and I count on when we are facing times of adversity and feel a real need for safety and a deliverer. But are you actually taking refuge in God's presence, in His stronghold? Part of our responsibility for our faith is to make our home in God's presence, not out in the world doing our own thing. Will you not only pray to God but also make your home your refuge with God? Don't just cry out to God; come home to God.

Chapter 38: "Lord, make me mindful of moments of temptation and your grace."

While 1 Peter 5:8 describes our enemy as a roaring lion, the temptations that come our way are often subtle and quiet. The serpent image of Genesis 3 fits the bill far more accurately in my life. How about you?

It is hard to know or imagine what scenarios or simple choices might lead someone to give in to temptations. One saying always reminds me that you cannot see the faults and flaws in a bridge until it collapses. In much the same way, you cannot see the flaws in a person's character until he or she meets with temptation.

One part of facing temptations is being mindful of ourselves. The idea of being mindful is the same as being aware. How well do you know yourself? Do you know, really and truly, those things that would tempt you? What would you be willing to take a step away from for God? What is it you want most in your life?

But that is only part of the prayer and how we face evil in ourselves. When James writes about resisting the devil in chapter 4, he also writes we are to submit ourselves to God. Why? Because God offers to us the powers of the Kingdom of God when we face temptations. We are given God's grace: strength and hope to resist those temptations seeking to lead us away from God.

This week, pray for mindfulness but not just for your weaknesses. Pray to be more mindful of the graces and gifts of God's presence made available to us every moment of every day.

Chapter 39: "Loving God, teach me to trust and keep me from harm."

"But the Lord is faithful, and He will strengthen and protect you from the evil one." – 2 Thessalonians 3:3

I always counted on my car to get me from point A to point B. For many years, it was faithful in its task. Then one day, the check engine light came on. When I took it in to be looked at, I discovered the problem. While the car had been faithful in its task, I had not been and had neglected to maintain the oil. I was without a car.

It would have been pointless to be upset with the car. It was a tool and had done its job as long as possible even while I was neglecting it. It cost me more than I wanted to pay, but I did learn the lesson.

The lesson was more than just about a car though. It is naïve for us to assume things will work even when we neglect to care for and maintain them. How much more so to think and live believing relationships with other people can be neglected by us and then blame others when we judge they failed us!

Prayer is an action we take that acknowledges God's place of priority in our lives. Trusting in a God we cannot experience with our five senses can be difficult at times, especially when we find our lives getting out of our control. But this is part of the issue: our lives and what happens are out of our control in many ways. Learning to trust in God doesn't guarantee bad things won't happen, but it does guarantee that God will not leave us or forsake us when bad things do happen.

Chapter 40: "In my shattered state my soul sits. Save me from sorrow and sin, Gracious Lord." (Psalm 62:1)

I got the call to come to church one afternoon. No reason was given, just for me to come. My home was the parsonage, and it didn't take more than a minute to get there. What I found when I arrived was a window that was shattered, and pieces were lying all around. It is always disappointing to come across something like that.

In many ways, our souls are like the window and shattered glass. Even though you and I are corrupted by our sin nature, our souls become the battleground. Our souls are created in the image of a holy and pure God, and a clean and clear window is a good analogy. When temptations come, they dirty the glass, make it difficult to see through, and shatter when you and I give in.

In the aftermath, who has the strength to clean it up? Who has the energy? Can we put the pieces back together as they were before? Sin shatters our souls and wounds us deeply each time. Even a "small" sin takes a toll.

But it is God's desire to forgive us and bring wholeness and healing to our souls! God promises He will never leave us or forsake us. God invites us to call out to Him to save us!

This breath prayer is a reflection of not only our needs but also the unique idea of a God full of grace, longing to give you a healing you do not deserve because He loves us and does not give up on us.

Chapter 41: "My God, my guide, make sure my next step."

"And the LORD will guide you continually and satisfy your desire in scorched places and make your bones strong; and you shall be like a watered garden, like a spring of water, whose waters do not fail." - Isaiah 58:11

I am a teacher. No, not in the more traditional sense of being in a classroom with a chalkboard or dry-erase board. I don't mean even in Sunday School classes. I love to teach what I know about the outdoors and being a sportsman. I love to teach tracking and taking people who have never been hunting to enjoy another side of God's creation most people miss.

Ever since my friend Jim took me turkey hunting for the first time when I was the associate pastor at his church, I have been fascinated by being able to have a "conversation" with wild turkeys. Learning to call them and track them is one of the most fun things I get to do. Getting to guide someone? I love it!

But turkeys are tricky and easily spooked. Taking someone into the woods for such an experience requires a guide to be attentive and patient and helping someone learn the woods with each step.

On our spiritual journeys, you and I will find we need to be guided, and there is no guide better for us than God. Hopefully, God's grace will bring us people who will help us hear God's Spirit, but ultimately, it is God who we need. Isaiah prophesies this for God's people, which applies to you and me as well. As you pray this breath prayer, listen carefully for God's voice and the ways in which God makes your way clearer.

Chapter 42: "Holy Spirit, quiet my mind so I might hear your voice."

Finding quiet places is not an easy thing to do in our world. I do love the conveniences technology allows us, but it is almost unreal when you think about it. We cannot go anywhere without our phones and people trying to reach us. For nearly 30 years of my life, I lived without a pager, cell phone, or a smartphone. My parents lived even longer, and my grandparents never lived to see that day!

But my kids can't remember such a time. They remember when they did not have one, but I'm not sure they can remember a time I did not. It is no wonder then that we struggle to find quiet places. There are so many voices and so much noise in our world and lives that finding time to be quiet is nearly impossible. Nearly.

Even two-thousand years ago, Jesus knew the pressure and noise of the crowds even before technology invaded the world. The Gospels all record something of Jesus' pattern of seeking solitude and quiet. Luke 5:15–16 records, "But now even more the report about him went abroad, and great crowds gathered to hear him and to be healed of their infirmities. But Jesus would withdraw to desolate places and pray."

The longer I have followed Jesus, the more I find I want to spend time in His presence. Being with God makes you desire more time. But it is not just in special times God wants to speak to you and me. No, it is God's desire to walk alongside and be present with us all throughout our day. It is God's desire to stay with us, not leave us or forsake us.

This breath prayer is an invitation to the Spirit of God to stay with us and speak to us often and always. Just as we know the voices of our friends and family without caller ID, the Spirit speaks, and you and I can come to know the voice of God.

Chapter 43: "Forgive me, Lord, so I can live forgiving."

"Then Peter came and said to Him, "Lord, how often shall my brother sin against me and I forgive him? Up to seven times? Jesus said to him, "I do not say to you, up to seven times, but up to seventy times seven."   Matthew 18:21-22

Growing up, I often heard the phrase after an argument, "Well, you need to bury the hatchet." That never seemed to make much sense to me, so I finally looked into its origin. It seems the phrase came from Native American tradition. Hatchets were actually buried by the chiefs of tribes when they came to a peace agreement.

I wasn't at all surprised when I came across this piece of advice: "When you bury the hatchet, don't bury it in your enemy's back." Far too often, this seems to be exactly what we do in our day and age. In so doing, we may destroy an enemy, but the "blood" remains on our hands and stains our hearts.

A theme throughout Jesus' teachings and sayings is this very topic of forgiveness. What Jesus points out though is that our willingness or unwillingness to forgive will always be tied to God forgiving or not forgiving us. It seems that forgiveness is the currency of the Kingdom of God. We cannot say we have love if we are unwilling to forgive those who have done us wrong.

Why would this be the case?

God forgave us when we didn't deserve it. Stop and let that sink in.

There may be nothing more telling about the condition of your heart than what you do with the power you have to forgive someone else. Giving and forgiving are two of the most significant marks of a Christian, for they represent the practical living out of love.

This breath prayer targets your heart and mine. To fully forgive and know its power, we need to know the power of God's forgiveness. Only then can we live forgiving others just as Jesus did and taught you and me to do.

Chapter 44: "This is your day, Lord. May my life show it."

"This is the day which the Lord has made; Let's rejoice and be glad in it." Psalm 118:24

When you read the words of the Psalm, if you have grown up going to church camp, you might start singing a song. Music has a way of getting into us. Good songs have a way of doing this to us. The Psalms are known as both the hymn book and prayer book of the Bible so it is no wonder we might burst out with a little song!

You say it. You sing it. You read it. Just because you echo and repeat the ancient words of scripture, the words don't become part of you by osmosis.

Our lives are meant to show out what God is doing. If you do see the day as one God made, rejoicing and being glad are a huge part of our response. What does it mean to you that God has made the day you are living? Why are you full of joy? Are you full of joy? What are you glad about? Are you glad at all? Do you see where I am going with this?

Take stock of life and the opportunity to be living and experiencing the day. There is much to be thankful but you need to attentive to what you are thankful for, what brings joy in it all and why you are glad. As you pray, may it become your soul's desire that this day God has made is a day when everyone you meet will rejoice and be glad because they meet up with you on this day!

Chapter 45: "Holy Spirit, speak clearly so I may hear and follow faithfully this year."

"I will ask the Father, and He will give you another Helper, so that He may be with you forever; the Helper is the Spirit of truth, whom the world cannot receive, because it does not see Him or know Him; but you know Him because He remains with you and will be in you."   John 14:16–17

"Selective hearing" is a wonderful thing both when you are a teenager and as a parent. As a kid, it got me out of chores many times, though it rarely got me out of trouble! As a parent, it allowed my children a few second chances to rethink some potentially poor decision-making. And for the record, I never for once thought that it was a good tactic for marriage (and I was right)!

And if there was ever an ongoing theme I hear as a pastor and spiritual director, it is the desire many people have to hear from God. So often, the desire is there, but people still miss out on hearing God. Is God not speaking? Are you not hearing Him? Or is it a combination of the two? Is it something altogether different you are missing out on?

The question I have is, "Do you really want to hear from God?" If you do, then you must be prepared to follow-up on what God does say to you. So, this breath prayer comes from my own desire to hear from God. This was my prayer during the first week of the new year in 2017, and it is my intent to pray it the first week of each year.

Jesus promised He would send to us a "counselor" who would be the "Spirit of truth." I gave up making New Year's resolutions each year because I failed to keep them. I am not always sure what is the best resolution to make each year, but I do know God is a God who desires the best for me.

I am also convinced that God is eager to speak. God made me and knows how to get through, so I put my trust in God to make known the way to go.

Chapter 46: "Lord, you know. Hear my every sigh."

"Lord, all my desire is before You; And my sighing is not hidden from You." Psalm 38:9

Doing "nothing" is a foreign concept in our world it seems. Maybe it has been this way for longer than we can imagine. I could harp on the temptations to be busy and on the go, and it is easy to blame technology on it all. It really matters little when it began. What matters is how we are living today.

I did not grow up hanging out with the old men at the front of a gas station in rocking chairs, but I know the image. I had trips with my dad and grandpa to co-ops and hardware stores where some of those times took place. The biscuit shops in north Georgia can sometimes house these gatherings.

After my wife's death, I found my front porch became a place where I could just sit and sigh. There seemed to be nothing else I could do, and few people understood. Even in the church/religious world, busyness and activity are the normal.

Maybe this is why fewer churches read Psalms in church? I wonder if these odd passages make us feel odd and out of sorts with God. We clergy preach about being more like Mary and less like Martha, but we still put a priority on getting everyone "plugged in" and doing a job.

You need to take time to sigh more.

And as those words become a prayer on our lips today and in the days ahead, you will grow more mindful of the reality of God's very real and very concerned presence for us and for the sighs we expel in our lives. Praying a breath prayer makes us aware of our breathing and the sighs we make. If God is aware of every sigh, surely He is aware of our deepest needs and concerns.

Rather than work more, try to sigh more.

Chapter 47: "Jesus, make me an attentive listener and a devoted follower."

"My sheep listen to My voice, and I know them, and they follow Me; and I give them eternal life, and they will never perish; and no one will snatch them out of My hand. My Father, who has given them to Me, is greater than all; and no one is able to snatch them out of the Father's hand. I and the Father are one."   John 10:27–30

I have always loved pets, even those I did not own. I have never been without one or more for many years. Right now, I have two cats who are learning and accepting becoming full-time indoor cats. Cats can be trained but for the most part, they prefer to do things their own way at their own time. Rarely do they follow commands.

Children and youth can have this problem, and adults are not immune to the struggle of listening either. Active listening is one of the first skills I work with when I do marital and premarital counseling.

Jesus makes it a point for followers of Him and seekers of God to be listeners. Jesus defines one of the most important characteristics of a Christian to be someone who both listens and follows His words. We don't get to pick and choose what we like and don't like about Jesus' teachings and claim, "I am Christian." We also do not get to give Jesus a mental nod and say, "Thanks. Got that. Love your enemy," and then go about seeking to put our enemy down and hurt them. We have to both hear and act.

This breath prayer is one to help us understand the importance of both of these in our lives of faith. Praying this prayer throughout our days can heighten our awareness of our need to be fully present so that we can hear Jesus' teaching and be more aware of others. Then we can do more than just listen to Jesus' words; we can begin to follow those words in our actions.

Chapter 48: "Our Father, keep me on the path of righteousness."

"I have instructed you in the way of wisdom; I have led you in upright paths."   Proverbs 4:11

Each of our faith journeys requires us to walk a path unique to us but common for all believers. I have loved hiking and backpacking for years now. When I go out with family and friends, I notice something important. We are all on the same trail, but I don't always step in the same place as those walking in front of me. Those behind me have their own stride too, so rarely do they step in the exact same spot I stepped. Yet we end up at the same destination.

We do not get to define what righteousness is. Through Scripture and the Church, we can find consistent teaching on righteousness, and it is something we dare not take lightly. In making this our prayer, we need to fully consider other terms like holiness, justice, love, purity, and others.

The path of righteousness is the same destination for all followers of Jesus Christ. Even so, it will be a different experience for each one of us. Our bodies and our burdens will affect the path we are each on.

We also should not forget the common thread we each share. Each time we pray the Lord's Prayer, when we say, "Our Father," we affirm a common faith. Praying "Our Father" in other prayers, like this one, connects us to this thread of faith we share in God.

Chapter 49: "O God, be Immanuel. Be with us. Be with me."

Every Advent, we hear the prophecy of Isaiah retold in Matthew's Gospel. We are reminded that the virgin will conceive and have a child, and the name of that child will be Immanuel. It is a name that means "God with us" (Matthew 1:23).

I've said it for years without giving it much thought. We're really talking about Jesus after all, and isn't *that* name the more important one?

During the first Advent after my late wife's diagnosis with cancer, I was missing any sense of a connection with God. I do not mean just a feeling about God but the assurance of my place with God. When the reading came up that Advent though, I heard God's voice reminding me, "Jesus is not the only name for the Messiah!" How true and powerful those words were to me!

The breath prayer for this week is a prayer regarding the dual nature of our relationship with Jesus. There is the public nature of that relationship that is often neglected: "God with us." Jesus came for the people of God, not only the nation of Israel but also Gentiles. Together, we are people of God, the Church.

And this is the second part of the prayer, "God be with me." While not a biblical and prophetic word, it remains nevertheless true. Our faith is personal, though not private. God knows the number of hairs on our heads.

How much more personal can we get? This is a God who fully embodies the name, "Immanuel."

This week, be open to God in your public worship and your personal time with God. As you pray this prayer, think of friends who are part of the journey. Don't stop there though. Consider those believers who you don't see eye to eye with. They too are part of the body of Christ, and Immanuel is here for them too.

Then consider your own personal connection with God. This is a week to plan for some time alone with God if you can. Maybe a special hike or visit to a favorite park. Maybe you need to schedule time to be at Adoration or to be in prayer at your church. Pray and listen this week.

Chapter 50: "Guide my children in your ways, O God."

"Train up a child in the way he should go, Even when he is old he will not depart from it." Proverbs 22:6

I have read a lot of books on parenting. There are so many opinions and approaches that it is laughable to consider them all, let alone point to one as *the* right way to parent a child.

The more I read and the longer I live as a parent, the more aware I have become of my limitations. There is only so much any one person can do. No matter how many times I tell my kids to study, they can make the decision to not study. They can be irresponsible with time and money, and I can take away driving privileges. I can tell them to not touch a hot stove, and yet, they may well do it anyway.

Each child is a person. Every person makes their own decisions—good or bad, wise or foolish, toward God or away from God. We do not own their hearts or their choices. In the end, no matter if it breaks our hearts or not, our children will choose the way they will go. Even if you do not have children of your own, I suspect there are children you care for too.

The breath prayer for this week is a prayer of intercession. It is an acknowledgment of our need for God and His part in the process, to undergird our children with grace. I do agree with the tenets of Proverbs 22:6, *and* I recognize God plays a role in what happens too!

We have limitations as parents. We have limitations as human beings. When we pray, it is an acknowledgment of our need for God and His intervention. It is by no means a magical incantation though! This prayer, to "guide my children…," is a plea, a request to One greater to help and empower our children in a way of life we believe to be the best.

We must not lose sight that this *is* a supernatural endeavor and practice! If we hold to the teachings of Scripture and the Church, God is Father. God knows the role parents must take and the responsibility the role carries. God not only knows it better than we do but also has known many more parents than we'll ever know! God the Father has heard cries similar to ours throughout the centuries.

In God, we have One who knows our worries and our work. Pray this breath prayer not only as intercession but also as a blessing, releasing your children and the children you love to the care of the One who loves them even more than you do.

Chapter 51: "Holy Spirit, quiet my mind so I might hear your voice."

"And [the angel] said, 'Go out and stand on the mount before the LORD.' And behold, the LORD passed by, and a great and strong wind tore the mountains and broke in pieces the rocks before the LORD, but the LORD was not in the wind. And after the wind an earthquake, but the LORD was not in the earthquake. And after the earthquake a fire, but the LORD was not in the fire. And after the fire the sound of a low whisper. And when Elijah heard it, he wrapped his face in his cloak and went out and stood at the entrance of the cave. And behold, there came a voice to him and said, 'What are you doing here, Elijah?'" 1 Kings 19:11–13

We live in an incredibly noisy world. I would say we are probably addicted to noise these days. I started using a small fan to help me sleep when I was younger and now use a white noise app on my phone to create the same sound. Am I covering up the silence, or do I really need some noise to soothe me to sleep?

Our lives seem to be going faster and faster with few signs of slowing down, and quiet only comes when we choose to turn the noise off and disconnect from our digital addictions. It would, of course, be nice to place the blame on someone else. We could try to point the finger in the direction of Microsoft, Apple, Android, Facebook, and the rest, but we all know we've wanted this! This is the advancement of technology.

We even put pressure on our churches and clergy to be engaged in technology so much so that they will stand outside in lines waiting for the new iPhone release (yes, I have clergy friends who have done this). Of course, I'm known for my own involvement in technology and social media, so I am not immune to the temptations of the hustle and bustle of it all. Noise and distractions come at us continually.

Of course, I have not even touched on the reality of life yet! How about parenting? And let's not forget work. Do you have a spouse or friends? What about the worries of house payments, car payments, insurance payments, the trip to the vet you've been putting off, and on and on? Our minds rarely find time to shut off and shut down. So, how will we ever hear the voice of God?

We pray.

We pray, and we take our concerns to the Spirit of God who indwells us and speaks to us. We come and implore the Spirit to quiet our minds. As the saints who have prayed the Jesus Prayer have observed, there is, in the repetition, a silencing of the mind. I can vouch for this in my own practice of praying the Jesus Prayer and these breath prayers. It is, after all, God's desire to speak to us and be in a relationship with us!

God is not playing games with us (though we may feel otherwise some days). The truth is that God is speaking to us early and often! There is so much God desires for us to know, like His wonders, but we need to listen to and learn the sound of the "low whisper" Elijah heard. This is the kind of prayer the Spirit longs to assist us in our faith journey, for it is the Spirit's role to bring us closer and closer to God.

Chapter 52: "Jesus, help me bear witness to your mercy and love."

Most of us like it when people like us. Maybe we are good at making people laugh or people know us as a good listener. It may even be that we are so good at certain things, people will even tell their friends about us. Typically, we refer to that as our reputation.

Proverbs 22:1 says that "A good name is to be chosen rather than great riches, and favor is better than silver or gold." The importance of a reputation is not a new invention of our culture and times. Once a good name is lost, it is difficult to reclaim, but I do not believe it is impossible. I have stood up for others' good names, and I have had to stand up for my own. It is not an issue of pride but of character.

What are you known for in your life? What is the witness that your life brings?

This breath prayer gets to the heart of the life of a follower of Jesus Christ. Look at it again. Read it slowly. Consider the scenario we live day by day as Christians.

There are over six billion people in the world. There are a few billion who have *never* heard about Jesus Christ. Not one word. Yet we say that we follow Jesus and desire to emulate Jesus' life and teachings in our own. What would our actions reflect about Jesus Christ? What reputation will Jesus have because of our lives?

Humbling, isn't it? Makes you a bit uncomfortable too? I get it. I feel the same way.

So then, look at this breath prayer. What exactly are we addressing in this prayer? For one thing, we are talking to Jesus. This prayer simply calls Jesus by His name. It represents a personal request and conversation. Jesus is the Son of God, and by His actions, we have been adopted into the family of God. In this way, Jesus is our "brother," so this is a personal request.

What we are acknowledging though is that we are in need of help. Like Peter in Matthew 14:22-33 when he is sinking, we cannot do this on our own! The Christian faith is not about trying harder and working our way to God by our own actions. We are dependent upon what Jesus has done for us. We know the mercy and love of God Almighty because of what Jesus has done for us.

Our lives are to bear witness to this mercy and love we have been shown. And yet, we know how difficult this is. How do we bear witness? How do we *tell* others about mercy and love if we don't *show* others mercy and love in our actions and words?

It doesn't always come easy to us either, does it?

A breath prayer is intended to "drill" down to the cry of our heart. It is not so easy to discern what the cry of our hearts might be though. Our hearts can be deceitful too, so we need to remember and listen carefully to the counsel of Scripture and the saints who have gone before us.

Chapter 53: "Jesus, open my ears to hear and eyes to see the least of these."

"...invite the poor, the crippled, the lame, the blind, and you will be blessed..." – Luke 14:13-14

As I mentioned before, I have lost part of my vision due to a rare vascular condition. My eyes still do their job, and I can still read, drive, hike, and hunt. Still, I miss some things in my traditional line of sight. What is funny is the times I don't see letters on a sign and what I see isn't what the sign says at all!

This is only one kind of vision, but not altogether different from today's prayer. I see, but I don't really see the need around me until it hits home. The least of these could be anyone. I don't know because I too often live with blinders on.

Is this a condemnation? No, it is a confession, and I need help taking out the log in my own eyes and the headphones that clog my ears from hearing the cry of the needy. There is hope!

The hope is found in the gift of God's presence. It is a hope found in the presence of friends in faith who care enough to help us with our failings. It is a hope found in the opportunities to be the hands and feet of Jesus to all those who are counted among the least of these (Luke 14:1, 7-14).

Chapter 54: "Spirit of God, abide in me."

"Be strong and courageous, do not be afraid or in dread of them, for the LORD your God is the One who goes with you. He will not desert you or abandon you." Deuteronomy 31:6

Loneliness is an incredibly debilitating feeling. During the pandemic of COVID-19, millions found themselves isolated, alone, and lonely. There were those who faced it for the first time during the many months of separation.

Scripture tells us God never leaves us or forsakes us, but there is a promise in the assurance of salvation that speaks even more pointedly to loneliness. Having the assurance of salvation is more than a promise God has given to you and me to comfort us until the end of the age. Paul tells us this promise is a sign of our adoption into the family of God (Romans 8:14–17). The words of Scripture offer the comfort of knowing you are a child of God, a part of God's family!

As you pray this prayer, remember these promises of God. God does not leave you guessing regarding your place in the family of God. You are God's child, and the Spirit will abide with you!

Chapter 55: How to Create Your Own Breath Prayer

Now that you have had some time practicing breath prayers, it is time to begin listening to the Spirit of God abiding in you and the longings of your heart. It is time to create your own prayers.

Faith is fun. I believe being in the presence of God and being engaged in an active vibrant faith, one can experience the best of life. Unfortunately, it seems, many have come to see faith as boring. "If we are bored by our own prayers, it is unlikely that God will be very interested in them," writes author and monk Simon Tugwell, in his book, *Prayer in Practice*[4]. I don't know if you have grown bored with faith, but breath prayers have changed my prayer life. It is my hope and prayer that if nothing else, you leave here with a prayer you are not bored to pray.

Much of the time, I think, we have a desire to want to keep the spiritual under our control. This isn't odd though because we generally like to keep everything under our control. In his class on the Old Testament, Dr. John Oswalt taught a great deal regarding the Ancient Near Eastern cult religions. All of these cults are based on the idea of man "discovering" gods and making sense of their world by rituals intended to control these gods.

But in the Judeo-Christian tradition, we have recorded it is God who initiated, God who reached out, and God who first loved. We understand Scripture to be a result of revelation, not evolution. The Wesleyan-Methodist

---

[4] Simon Tugwell, *Prayer in Practice.* Springfield, Illinois, Templegate Publishers, 1974.

concept of "prevenient grace," the grace that "goes before," makes this a vital foundation to prayer: God speaks first. What we do is a response to God's action. And the conversation that begins between us and God? That is prayer.

In his book *Shattered Dreams*, Dr. Larry Crabb makes this observation: "It is in the pain that we discover our desire for God."[5] Now, pain can take on *many* forms. The pain that drives us toward God maybe related to work, family, faith, or health, and the list goes on. For me, you can combine all of these and a few more, but none was so transformative as being my wife's caregiver and living through her death from colon cancer after a twenty-month battle with the disease.

Pain and prayer have gone hand in hand for some time. And in observing the life of Jesus and the lives of the saints, both those who lived by the Law of the Old Covenant and those who followed Jesus after the New Covenant, we find their spiritual lives governed by a more simple spirituality. Jesus sums up the Law this way:

> "And one of them, a lawyer, asked him a question to test him. 'Teacher, which is the great commandment in the Law?' And he said to him, 'You shall love the Lord your God with all your heart and with all your soul and with all your mind. This is the great and first commandment. And a second is like it: You shall love your neighbor as yourself. On these two commandments depend all the Law and the Prophets.'" – Matthew 22:35–40 ESV

---

[5] Larry Crabb, *Shattered Dreams: God's Unexpected Path to Joy*, Colorado Springs, Waterbrook Press, 2001.

As part of my first 5 Day Academy of Spiritual Formation in 2011, we were encouraged to read "The Way of A Pilgrim." It is a spiritual classic from the Orthodox tradition of the church. It tells the story of a pilgrim who learns to pray the Jesus Prayer: "Lord Jesus Christ, Son of God, have mercy on me, a sinner." The pilgrim's learning to pray this prayer took place as he walked and journeyed. I began praying it and found it a wonderful gift and way to pray.

My daughter, Jay, and I were planning to start section hiking in the summer of 2014. We had planned to do 50 miles of the Georgia section of the Appalachian Trail that first time out. In preparation, I debated about what to carry—namely to take a Bible and/or devotional. But it was "The Way of a Pilgrim" that won out. No, I didn't take the book. I took the narrative—I simply took the practice of the Jesus Prayer.

Up and down the mountains of the Appalachian Trail, I prayed the Jesus Prayer: "Lord Jesus Christ, Son of God, have mercy on me, a sinner." That was it. But what began happening was far more personal and transformative. I began to breathe it in and out and meditate on each phrase and then each word. The rhythm of my feet, my heart, my mind, and my soul came to resonate with it. This is what the pilgrim spoke about—coming to "pray without ceasing."

Abba Matoes, one of the early desert fathers of the church, said, "The nearer a man draws to God, the more he sees himself a sinner. It was when Isaiah the prophet saw God that he declared himself 'a man of unclean lip' (Isaiah 6:5)." It is hard to miss that truth over the many steps taken saying you are a sinner.

It is also hard to miss the power and magnificence of the word "mercy." Just that one word becomes a prayer too. And suddenly, you have the basis for another form of Simple Prayer called "Centering Prayer." Referring to the book *The Cloud of Unknowing*, Simon Tugwell describes how powerful a one-word exclamation can be. "Fire!" yelled by someone running from a burning home is sufficient for a response. Consider simply "Amen" and how with its traditional definition to mean "So be it" or "I agree" or "Lord, make it so," it becomes a prayer. Pick any word found in Scripture—love, peace, patience, faith, hope, grace, Jesus, Savior, Spirit—and each word, like mercy, holds a multitude of prayers to be considered.

In just a few moments, we'll work on a simple pattern for creating your own breath prayer. My first breath prayer that I used for some time was "Our Father, my God, grant me you." But when my wife's diagnosis came, this prayer seemed so lacking, and I chose to go back to praying the Jesus Prayer. And it was in this stepping back into the practice of the Jesus Prayer that I saw it as a way to *intercede* for others, especially my wife: "Lord Jesus, have mercy on Heather." I would add my kids to my prayers in this way.

I didn't have to think of words to say. They came over and over again. Why? It was the practice of being on the trail. By this time, I was using an Orthodox Prayer Rope and then prayer beads.

When Heather and I received the news that her cancer was not responding to the chemotherapy, we were both heartbroken. As I prayed, I found something new rising in me, and from it came a new breath prayer:

"Jesus, have mercy and grant me comfort." It too became a prayer of intercession for Heather and our kids. Most days, my prayer boiled down to "Jesus, have mercy" or "Mercy, Lord."

And this began a pattern of listening to the Spirit more regularly for how I might pray. What is it that I feel or experience a burden for? It is not just from my heart either, as the Psalms and other Scriptures also provide guidance for how I might pray.

These steps are nothing magical. If you're attentive to God's voice, you may find breath prayers coming from other sources. Scripture will be one, but so will other prayers of the Church and from journal writing you might do. Don't hesitate to go back through this book and examine the prayers again. What names of God resonate with you? What prayers or words catch your heart? Let's go through the steps.

1. **SIT** with God

Find a good time and space where you seem to most connect with God. The Spirit of God can speak anywhere, and sitting with God may include other activities. It is just a way of saying "be aware" of God.

2. **SENSE** God speaking

Ignatius of Loyola was a big proponent of using our imagination in spiritual practice. Imagine God is asking you, "What do you want?" But listen carefully too. God may also be asking you to pray something specifically. God may say, "This is what you are to pray," or, "Look for my words to your prayer."

3. **SHARE** with God

This is practicing "active listening" with God. Whether it is a word like "mercy" or "forgiveness" that comes from a Bible verse, what resonates with your soul? This is largely the time of forming the core of your prayer based on what the Spirit is speaking to you.

4. **SPEAK** God's name

What is the name of God that fits best your prayer? Ron DelBene encourages a person to think of a favorite name, but I try to consider the wealth of names that are available or the one that fits the tone or meaning of the prayer. "Savior" may not be as significant as using "Spirit," for example, depending on your prayer.

5. **SETTLE** on a prayer

Here, you put it together: the prayer with the name of God. Speak it out loud. Chew on it quietly. Consider its rhythm and where God's name fits best. Be willing to change it as you continue to pray it and learn from God.

That's it! Nothing more. I often use an app on my phone to write out my own breath prayers, but other times, I use a blank piece of paper to do the creative work. More than anything, I hope you'll learn and grow and come to know God in new and exciting ways as you learn to breathe. But I won't just leave you hanging. On the next page, I'm giving you some space to work on your own breath prayers, and some cues to help you on your journey in prayer.

Questions to help	Make notes from the questions
Which prayers resonated with you?	
What names for God do you prefer?	
Imagine God asking you, "What do you want?"	
What Bible verse comes to your mind?	

Take the notes above and use this space to work on creating a breath prayer. Come back to this space anytime. Remember, this is YOUR breath prayer!

What did you think?

Thank you for purchasing and reading *Prayer: Simply Breathe*. There are a lot of books out there on prayer and many of them are good, but you picked this one and for that I am eternally grateful!

If this book has been an encouragement and help on your spiritual journey with God, would you take 5 minutes and write a review on Amazon? When you do, you offer important feedback for my writing and ministry. I want to be sure what I give is of value to you the reader and honors the gifts God has given.

Do no harm, do good, and stay in love with God! This is the Way!
Ken L. Hagler, aka: Jedi Pastor Ken

www.kenhagler.com
@jedipastorken

About

Ken has been in ministry for nearly three decades as a youth pastor, pastor, and spiritual director. During that time, Ken has been writing and creating content encouraging people to live their faith for everyday. Online, Ken is known as "Jedi Pastor Ken" and creates videos, breath prayer graphics and blogs to guide people as they follow God. Ken is a graduate of Asbury Theological Seminary and Garrett Evangelical Theological Seminary. He has also completed the Upper Room Two Year Academy for Spiritual Formation. *Prayer: Simply Breathe* is Ken's third book and second book on spiritual practices. Ken lives in Alaska with his wife and together, they enjoy the adventure of life and of faith.

Printed in Great Britain
by Amazon